best wishes

DANNY BOY

by Danny Crates & Jon Cudby

First published in March 2012

© Written by Danny Crates & Jon Cudby

© Pictures - Danny Crates, Getty Images and Pure Image Photography

© Cover pic - Getty Images

© Design - Mpress (Media) Ltd

ISBN NUMBER 978-0-9570398-4-1

Designed and published by m press (Media) LTD.

Unit Four, Ashton Gate, Harold Hill, Romford, RM3 8UF

Dedication

Dedication

I would like to dedicate this book to my two wonderful sons Henry and Albert. You have made my life complete.

Also my wife Victoria, mum, dad and brother, Paul, you have all helped shape the person I am and always been there to support and guide me through the good and bad times.

The title, "Danny Boy", I dedicate to my mum. I know whenever she hears the song it brings a tear to her eye. I would like to think it is all the happy endearing memories it conjures up. In reality it is probably the pain and anguish I have caused her during my life.

Acknowledgements

Acknowledgements

Jon Cudby
This story would never have made it onto paper without my writer, Jon Cudby. I have dreamt of turning the story I tell on stage into a book for many years, but never found anyone who could help me achieve it. Who would have thought that person would turn out to be my cousin? Thank you for making my dream come true.

Thurrock Rugby Club
The support from the club and players gave me the strength to rebuild my life after losing my right arm at just 21 years old.

Victoria
My wife, Victoria, has had to deal with the ups and downs that my career has dealt me, usually on a daily basis. Thank you for supporting the many choices I have had to make. Victoria would be the first to tell you that life with an athlete is never easy.

Henry and Albert
My two boys have helped me remember that, above all my dreams and aspirations, life should be about fun. And chocolate!

I would like to thank my mum, dad and brother Paul for all the support and love you have shown me, especially after my accident, while I was struggling to find myself again.

Ayo Falola
My coach, Ayo, took me on as a wayward 26-year-old and turned me into an international athlete. Thank you for your support, patience and guidance.

Chris Phillips
For his continued coverage during my athletics career, and his input into the first few chapters of this book.

Last, but no means least, I want to thank my many friends, too many to name in the book, who have stood by every decision I have made, picked me up when life has knocked me down, and brought me back if ever I lost my way.

It is not possible to name everyone that has touched my life, for that I am sorry, but you are by no means forgotten.

Contents

Foreword

Lord Sebastian Coe
Foreword

I first met Danny many years ago, when he was achieving great success as an athlete in the 800m – an event close to my heart.

I then got to know him really well as a person when Danny made such a valuable contribution as an ambassador for our London 2012 bid team.

Who can forget that iconic image of him leaping for joy alongside Steve Cram and Kelly Holmes in Trafalgar Square as Jacques Rogge announced that the Olympics would be coming to London?

Danny's 12-year international Paralympic career included many titles and spanned three Paralympic games. First, he returned to Australia – the scene of his life-changing accident – to take bronze in the Sydney games. Gold in Athens then followed before Beijing, where Danny proudly carried the flag in the opening ceremony before injury cruelly robbed him of the chance to compete.

Off the track, Danny is still excelling and has used his retirement from athletics to develop his career as a public speaker, both on the corporate, after-dinner circuit and in schools, giving motivational talks to children.

As an accomplished speaker, his audiences often tell him that his personal odyssey should be turned into a book. I am delighted that he has taken their advice to pursue his natural storytelling ability and do just that.

This is not a standard autobiography about another sportsperson achieving their dreams. This is a rollercoaster of emotions, from the young Essex boy with his whole life ahead of him, who loses an arm in a car crash, to the long journey of overcoming that trauma to establish himself as a world-beating athlete.

There are the highs and lows of a life in competition and then, finally, the tough decision to retire as Danny embraces a life after running.

Through all this, Danny maintains the unique sense of humour and incredible optimism that makes this such a captivating story.

Chapter 01
No hurdle in life is impossible to overcome

I regained consciousness at the bottom of a 15-foot embankment in the driver's seat of a wrecked car.

Moments earlier I had been enjoying the drive to Airlie Beach in Queensland, Australia, looking forward to catching up with old friends one last time before returning home to England at the end of what had been the most amazing year of my life.

How had I got here? Had I hit another car? Or lost control of mine? All these thoughts running through my mind distracted me from the fact that my arm was starting to hurt.

I looked down and saw a severed arm lying across my lap. At first I was scared it was from a pedestrian or another car I had collided with. I did not even contemplate that it might be mine.

In a state of panic, I turned to my passenger, Barry, for reassurance, but all he said was, "Don't look down, it's your arm." I don't know why but those words seemed to calm me.

I tried to get out of the car, but it had sustained a lot of damage and the door on my side was wedged shut. Barry was already clambering out of the window on his side and I followed close behind, a scared 21-year-old carrying his own severed arm.

As I saw Barry scrambling up the bank, I was suddenly alone, scared and slipping into shock. Just at that moment my guardian angel arrived in the form of a woman called Cathy. She had heard the crash from her house and came to see what had happened.

At this point, although I had seen the arm, I had not registered how bad the situation was, so the fact that I was losing blood at a frightening rate was not a concern to me – I was more interested in climbing up the embankment.

But Cathy could see the danger I was in and ran across, wrestling me to the ground with the sort of tackle that would have made the Australian rugby team proud. The only way she could keep me still was to sit on me while we waited for the ambulance.

It is funny but I felt exactly the way you see in films when someone is in trouble – my eyes were closing and I had an overwhelming desire to sleep. Thankfully Cathy was determined to be annoying and did everything she could to keep me awake.

From nowhere I turned to Cathy and said, "I think I have stuffed my rugby career."

It must have been one of the hardest things for her to hear that and have to lie, but she told me I would be fine and back playing in no time, although she didn't need to be a doctor to see that my arm was unsavable.

While I hadn't felt the pain at first, I was definitely feeling it now, an unbearable burning sensation in my right shoulder. Finally, I heard the sound I had been waiting for, and Cathy had no doubt been praying for – sirens. Help had arrived.

The fire brigade was first on the scene and they quickly noticed a strong smell of petrol coming from the car. Without pause for breath I was fastened to a stretcher and run up the hill. Bizarrely, through all that was happening and the pain I was in, I remember smiling at the fact that, in their haste, the fire crew were carrying me the wrong way – feet first – up the hill, so I kept sliding off the board while they frantically tried to hold me in place.

By the time we reached the top of the bank the ambulance had arrived. All I remember at that point was asking to be put to sleep. Of course this was not possible – all they could offer me was gas and air for pain relief.

Meanwhile, the driver of the other vehicle involved in the collision – a 74-year-old local farmer – was 100 yards up the road, casually changing the tyre on an otherwise unscathed car. Once his tyre was changed, he left without even coming to see if I was all right.

All this had happened in a small town called Sarina, about 40 miles south of Mackay, and luckily it was only a few miles to the local hospital. My last memory is lying on the table while the doctor unwrapped the bandage now holding my arm in place. I don't know if I lost consciousness or they put me to sleep, but I recall nothing of my second ride in an Australian ambulance – the transfer to Mackay Base Hospital, where I would receive the specialist attention I needed.

Again, my memory of this time is vague. My only recollection is of a doctor explaining that they would do all they could to save the arm, but there was a chance they would have to amputate or, as I like to say, "finish what I started".

The doctor asked for my permission to amputate if needed. I replied sharply, "I don't care, just put me to sleep." Then the lights went out. Relief at last.

While I was under the knife, unbeknown to me, someone had made the phone call that every parent dreads: "Mrs. Crates, your son has been involved in a serious accident." I can only imagine the fear my mum felt as she passed the phone to my dad, unable to comprehend what was happening. They received the call at 4am so were unable to do anything until the morning and must have felt totally alone.

First thing next morning, Dad was on a train to London to get visas; Mum, with the help of a friend, was throwing clothes into a suitcase. Within 12 hours of hearing the news, they were on a flight bound for Sydney, still over a day away from seeing their son, not knowing how bad his injuries were. For two smokers, that flight would have been a very anxious 24 hours.

I was now conscious enough to start realising what had happened to me. The bandaged stump gave it away, even if my brain could not quite register. I spent the next 24 hours in a morphine-induced state, slipping in and out of consciousness.

Next came one of the most welcome but difficult situations of my life. I was informed that my parents had arrived, just 36 hours after my accident. Bearing in mind the flight took up 24 hours of that time, I still find it incredible that they got there so quick. Luckily they had friends who lived just a few miles from the hospital, so Roger and Jackie were able to offer Mum and Dad a base, as well as some much needed support.

As my parents walked into the room, I broke down for the first time since the accident. While totally devastating, seeing me awake must have been some sort of relief for them. Until that moment, they'd had no way of knowing how bad I was.

This was the first time I had seen my parents for just over a year, and it wasn't the reunion any of us had planned, but at that moment it was a reunion we were all glad to see.

The next four days were pretty mundane, all things considered. Mum and Dad came and went and I slept a lot, mostly due to losing half of my blood in the accident. The doctor explained that I had been borderline for a transfusion.

I now had the choice, if I had the transfusion, I would regain strength quicker, but if I let the blood levels increase naturally I would have to wait to return home until I was strong enough to fly. It was no contest. Even in that condition, I would take any excuse to extend my stay in Australia.

The news that a young Brit had been involved in an accident had quickly travelled Australia and reached my friends at home, so the hospital was inundated with calls. As soon as they had hung up each one, the phone would ring again. Friends always have a way of cheering you up when the chips are down. Not one of them asked how I was coping or anything like that. All I got was comments like: "You dozy prat, we always said you were a rubbish driver!" The kind of comments only your mates could make, and still make you laugh.

Even with friends back home lifting my spirits while I recovered, it became apparent to the nurses that I wasn't acknowledging my amputation, so they arranged a visit from a local amputee they knew.

His advice was simple: get the nurse to close the curtains and remove the bandage, then look at the stump in my own time. It was truly heart-wrenching and for a long time I could not bring myself to look, but eventually I plucked up the courage. It was much cleaner than I expected, the skin was stretched over the end and stitched at the back.

Only 10 stitches too. To be honest I felt a bit cheated – I would have got more stitches if I'd fallen off of my bike. I was grateful for the advice though, because as hard as it was to accept the amputation, I now at least had a visual image of what it looked like.

During my hospital stay, I also received a visit from the local police, firstly to question me and then to formally charge me with crossing the white line and causing the accident, the charge based on the fact that broken glass from my car was found on the opposite side of the road. The police's visit was greeted with resentment from me, my family and the nursing staff, who fairly bluntly asked them to leave.

By about day five I was getting back to my old self. One of the highlights of my day was being given a shower by three of the nursing staff. Then came the news I did not want to hear – the ward sister told me I was well enough to shower myself. It might have taken me a couple of days to pass on that particular message.

I quite enjoyed my time in hospital, as strange as that may sound, but there were some harsh realities to be learned. I had to learn to dress myself with one arm, and my left one at that.

By day six I was doing well enough to persuade my doctor to let me out for lunch with my parents. I was even allowed one beer, although I had to promise it would only be a light one.

On the way to lunch, we were walking through a shopping centre. I couldn't get a t-shirt or shirt over my bandage so I was wearing a vest with the bandaged stump clearly visible for all to see.

For the first time I was aware of people staring at me. In all honesty, they were just doing what I would probably have done myself in their position. Generally the attention was motivated by curiosity and was not malicious, although I did get the odd comment. It was just something else I would have to learn to accept – I would face it for the rest of my life – but it took a number of years for me to really get used to it.

By day eight I was allowed out for the weekend, and with the aid of my parents I finally made it to Airlie Beach and the friends I had been on the way to see just over a week before.

I think that weekend was a huge relief to my parents. From that point they realised that, although it was going to be tough, I would be OK. From my point of view, it gave me great pleasure to introduce my parents to the friends I had grown to love so much.

It was then back to the hospital to be formally discharged, only 10 days after the accident. But before they released me back into the big wide world, I had the formality of seeing the hospital psychologist.

After a brief assessment she explained what I was likely to go through over the next couple of years. As if losing my arm was not enough, she explained I might endure a period of anger, followed by questioning – "why did this have to happen to me?" – and then depression could set in. I wished I hadn't asked.

So on the 10th day I was discharged, with not much from my hospital stay to boast about considering the condition I was left in. Four hours on the operating table, only 10 stitches and out of hospital after just 10 days.

In the build-up to the accident I had been doing some work for a Brisbane-based backpackers' hostel called the Swagman's Rest. It wasn't the most reputable of establishments, but it was a way to earn some much-needed money to pay for a new flight home. I did have a ticket but I had let it expire and become invalid. Oh, the days of being totally irresponsible.

One of the final jobs was to travel up the coast from Brisbane to Airlie Beach with the manager, Barry, distributing flyers for the hostel. Looking back, undertaking a 600-mile journey might not have been the most intelligent thing I have done in my life, but there was an added incentive – Airlie Beach had been my home for the best five months of a brilliant year in Australia, and I couldn't resist the opportunity to visit it one last time.

Because I had been working at the time of the accident I was advised to apply for worker's compensation, so we went to the appropriate office to lodge our claim. Surprisingly to us they could not find any records of The Swagman's Rest, but they assured us this was probably an error with their system and that they would look into it.

Before we left for Brisbane to meet with the owner of the hostel, we had some important stops to make. First and most important was a visit to Cathy, the lady who had given me so much immediately after the accident. It was an incredible feeling, being able to thank someone for being there when I was so alone and in danger. It was interesting to hear her side of the story: how she had heard the cars collide from her house, how she felt when she saw the condition I was in, and her relief when the ambulance finally arrived.

Cathy's husband picked up the story: apparently she had refused the ambulance crew's request to attend hospital for a check up. But when she got home and in the shower to wash off the blood, she broke down uncontrollably. The crew had known such a reaction was likely and, Sarina being a small town, they came back to Cathy's house to check on her after they had dropped me off. Ultimately she had to be taken to hospital.

How could I even begin to thank Cathy, knowing that what she had done for me had such an impact on her, leaving her with her own demons to deal with from the accident?

Then it was off to see the site where I had the crash. Not much there really, just a ditch and a few tyre tracks, although I don't quite know what I expected. Next came the tough one as we went to see the car. What a job I had done! I don't think that will be back on the road.

To be honest I don't know what I thought as I saw the damage and the blood inside. Was I lucky to be alive, or unlucky to have had the crash? I am an optimist in life, but sometimes you have to wonder which way round my luck actually went that day. Let's stick to lucky to be alive.

Next it was down to Brisbane and the owner of the Swagman's Rest to explain that I might have dented his car. We talked about the accident and what would happen next. He was shocked to hear that we had applied for worker's compensation. As we then found out, he had not been declaring his staff.

He arranged for us to meet his solicitor, who agreed to handle my case and explained that the worker's compensation was nothing to worry about: the insurance settlement would more than cover that. In the light of day, alarm bells should have been ringing at this point, but when you consider the state of shock my family and I had found ourselves in, it is not surprising we missed the signs.

Before I could leave for home I had to clear a medical bill. Two days before starting the journey to Airlie Beach, I had been involved in a bit of a disagreement with another member of staff, the result being that he got a black eye, which I dislocated the middle finger of my right hand giving him (although, to be fair, I got a split lip myself). My finger had needed to be reset in hospital.

As we walked back into the hospital two weeks later to settle my bill, the clerk behind the desk could not believe what she was seeing. I was paying for treatment on a finger I no longer had. She didn't let me off the fee though.

Because there would eventually be an insurance claim the amputation had to be medically documented – apparently it is not enough to just show you have lost an arm – so off we went to see the relevant doctor, who looked at and measured the stump, and happily charged us $400 for the privilege. From that moment on, my parents realised that anything to do with the case would be expensive. If only I had listened to them and taken out travel insurance for my trip, but back then a year's cover was expensive, so I'd decided I had better things to spend the money on.

Then, finally, came the moment we had all been waiting for. Just four weeks after the accident I was ready to fly home. The journey went well. There was a little panic for my parents and flight crew as my face started to glow red soon after take-off, but luckily it soon settled down and we managed a relatively incident-free flight back to Britain.

When we got home we were greeted my younger brother Paul's wrecked car in the driveway. He was only 19 and had been left home alone while Mum and Dad flew to Australia. He was going through college at the time and couldn't join them, which must have been tough for him. While they were visiting me, he had driven his Orion Ghia – another good Essex boy car – through a wall.

He hadn't told Mum and Dad, thinking that coping with one son's car crash might be enough for them to deal with. The first they knew of his accident was when they arrived at the house and saw the state of his car – quite a welcome. Luckily Paul didn't have any serious injuries, just a wounded pride.

I had only gone to Australia in the first place as a result of another crash. Early in 1993 someone ran into the back of my car while I was sitting at a junction. Once the insurance agreed I was not at fault and paid out I had the car repaired, but only three days later another car pulled out in front of me and once again I had wrecked my car. The second accident happened just 100 metres from the first. Both times I had been going to the same mate's house – Paul Greene.

As soon as the second claim was settled, I decided to take the money and go to Australia. I figured bad luck often happens in threes, so I would be better off going traveling rather than take the chance of a third crash...

Chapter 02
A happy childhood

Those three crashes were far from my first accidents. I was always an accident-prone child and one of my earliest memories is my mum and dad buying me this big, purple tricycle when I was about three, only for me to ride it straight off the raised patio in our garden and crack my chin open.

I was taken to hospital where Dad had to hold me up on the bed while they stitched my chin back together. Mum always likes to tell the story that the nurse came out to tell her that her three-year-old son was absolutely fine, but that her husband had passed out.

That trip to hospital was just the first of many, but despite all the mishaps and injuries, I had a very happy childhood.

I was born on 9 February 1973 in Orsett, Essex, and was followed two years later by my brother Paul. We've always got on well, and never really fought as kids. We both had a love of sports and our parents were constantly driving us all over the place for judo, rugby, football, athletics or whatever we were into at the time.

Our active side probably came from my mum, Sheila, who was very sporty when she was younger. Before having children, she worked for a bank in London while my dad, Brian, was a merchant seaman before becoming a lorry driver. I was too young to really remember, but he was away a lot in the lorry and worked every hour under the sun to make ends meet.

My parents weren't rich and we never had the best of anything but they did everything they could for us. Every year we would go away on holiday, taking our trailer tent to Wales or Devon or Cornwall to spend two weeks in the rain. Paul and I had a great time, but it probably wasn't much fun for my parents. Pretty soon, Dad got fed up with the bad weather and decided to drive us to the South of France or Spain every year instead.

It took 24 hours to get there, which wouldn't have been much of a holiday for a lorry driver, even without me and Paul screaming in the back seat. Even so, the break was something we all looked forward to every year. Although now I'm a caravan-owner with two young kids of my own, the memory of those holidays doesn't really suggest 'rest and relaxation' to me.

When I reached school age, I went to Giffards Primary in Corringham. I never really took to the academic side of school and spent most lessons messing around or just looking out of the window, wishing I was outside playing.

From a young age, most of my reports said I was quite chatty, always wanting to be the centre of attention, and that I would have been capable of doing a lot better if I would only put as much energy into studying as I did into clowning around in class. But I had no interest in doing better academically. Even at primary school, it was all about sport for me.

I still remember my first PE teachers at Giffards – Mr. Davies and Mr. Richards. Like all PE teachers in the 1980s they were both Welsh and it was them who first encouraged me to get more involved with sport.

They introduced me to rugby and I took to it straight away. I even played for the fourth years' team when I was still a year below. The rugby pitch was where I excelled, but I also represented the school at athletics, cricket and football.

It was Mr Davies and Mr Richards who persuaded me to take my rugby and athletics to the next level and encouraged me to join my local club. By the age of 10 I had joined Thurrock Rugby Club and was running for Thurrock Harriers.

My rugby went from strength to strength, but I found the step up in athletics difficult. I had been regularly winning events at my school sports day and in district school athletics competitions, but with the Harriers I quickly got used to seeing my team-mates come out on top.

I trained with some amazing athletes, including Adam Brainwood, Robert Peacock and the Gerrard brothers, Peter and David. Much as I enjoyed being with the Harriers, I was always in the shadows and had no aspirations of ever becoming an athlete myself. For me, athletics was all about having fun and I was happy just to run along with them.

I did have one moment of glory with the Harriers though. At the age of 12 I won the district 1500 metres – my first and only district sports medal. My granddad, Bob was in hospital at the time and I remember my parents saying how my victory had made his day. Sadly he died two weeks later.

Like my other granddad, Chris, who had also died four years previously, Bob was fiercely competitive. Both men had boxed in the army and it's probably them I have to thank for the will to win I developed later in life. I lost both my grandfathers at a young age, but I like to think they would both have been proud to see that I eventually inherited some of their competitive spirit.

I won a few medals below district level, but nowhere near as many as my team-mates who were breaking club records, winning counties championships and getting selected to represent the South of England.

Competitively I only ran, but I used my time at Thurrock to try my hand at everything, from the hammer to the high jump. By the time I left Giffards to go on to secondary school I was into athletics as much as I was rugby.

I went on to Gable Hall Comprehensive in Corringham, which had a reputation for being quite rough but was the best of a bad bunch in my area and was improving. A new headmaster called Mr. Jones had just taken over and he had only just introduced school uniform, although there were still kids who didn't wear it.

Luckily for me there was a heavy focus on sport and I made sure I had the PE teachers onside from the start. The best advice I can give any youngster is to be nice to your PE teachers because you never know when you might need them.

Just like in primary school I often found myself in trouble for talking too much during lessons. One time I had been through several final warnings in a maths lesson before the teacher told me I would be in detention that night, when I was due to play rugby.

I protested, "But, Miss, we've got quite a big game on!"

She insisted. I was in detention and would just have to miss the game that night. News of this obviously got to the staff room and, five minutes later, one of the PE teachers, Mr Power, came in and whispered in her ear. I don't know what he said but she quickly turned my detention into another final warning.

Academically, maths and physics were the only subjects I actually enjoyed. I hated chemistry and biology and was always being sent out of English lessons for talking. I couldn't get geography at all but, to be honest, I didn't really apply myself in any of these subjects.

I also developed a mischievous streak as a teenager, although it was more a cheeky side than ever getting into real trouble. When I was about 14 I sneaked out of scout camp to go to the pub with some girls. I'd got out with a mate called Kevin Bourne and we had a great night.

We thought we'd got away with it, but when we climbed over the wall to come back, the light on the roof of the minibus suddenly came on. We froze in its beam, sitting on top of the fence, one leg each side, startled like rabbits in the headlights.

The scoutmaster had waited up after spotting we were missing and was waiting, ready to catch us as soon as we came back.

We were both sent home early as a punishment, so the next morning my mum had to come and pick me up. It was a fairly quiet journey home.

Another time, I'd been out with my mate Paul Greene and we'd brought a couple of girls back to his house at 4 o'clock in the morning. As naïve young boys we decided that board games would be the best form of entertainment so we crept into his parents' bedroom looking for a Monopoly set.

We were not as quiet as we thought and I can still remember the startled look on his mum's face as she woke with a fright to see her son and his mate on all fours, rummaging through her wardrobe in the darkness.

I was still involved in rugby at school, but I stopped playing for Thurrock and left the Harriers too as my out-of-school activities started to revolve more around mucking about with my mates.

As a result, my exam grades suffered. I got a B and two Cs in my GCSEs. The rest were Ds and Es. I did all right but it was an Essex comprehensive school in the 1980s and they didn't churn out too many rocket scientists. That's my excuse anyway.

I left school at 16 and started an apprenticeship, training as an engineer with Mobil Oil. I'd had other offers from Ford and Shell, but Mobil was based at Coryton Refinery, near where I lived, so that swung it.

The first year of the apprenticeship was spent at Thurrock Technical College, studying the basics of engineering. I then came back to do day release for another two years, spending four days a week doing on-the-job training at the refinery. I absolutely loved it.

Midway through those last two years, I had to choose a trade. I wanted to be a mechanic even though people were trying to put me off, telling me mechanical engineering was a dying trade. Everyone I worked with told me electrical or instrument engineering would be the sensible way to go and would take me further in life, but I was 18 and just wanted to play with big tools and get greasy.

They also said that bashing things with hammers and getting dirty might lose its appeal after a few years, but I was a cocky teenager and wouldn't listen. So I spent the last year of my apprenticeship focusing on mechanical engineering.

Around this time I passed my driving test and got my first car. I had been taught by a friend of the family, but not before I'd also tried being taught by my dad. At the end of the first – and last – lesson with him I'm not sure which of us was more relieved to rip the L plates off the car, but it's safe to say we never went out for a driving lesson together again.

After passing, I got a Mark One Ford Escort, which my Uncle Barry had lovingly restored for me, only for me to repay him by reversing it into a tree.

While doing the apprenticeship I also rediscovered my love of rugby and went back to Thurrock at the age of 16 or 17 to play for their colts team. I played on the wing and soon I had made it into the Essex and Eastern Counties sides at under-18s level.

I went on tour to Cheshire with the Eastern Counties team and actually won the Man of the Tour award. A lot of the players in that team went on to enjoy successful professional rugby careers and that was fast becoming my dream too.

However, while I was on that tour, convincing myself that everything was now set for me to achieve that dream, a winger who had been away at private school came back and walked straight back into the team at my expense. I found myself relegated to the bench and didn't play for the Eastern Counties again until the last game of the season.

Despite the setback, I carried on with the colts at Thurrock for the next two years. I got myself into the Essex under-21s team and, at the age of 20, I made it into Thurrock's first team, scoring a try on my debut.

We were trained by this big Kiwi, Hicker Reed, who had been a fairly notorious hooker for the All Blacks during his playing career. He had lost none of his power to intimidate and we were a well-drilled team, but I was loving the game again and everything was going really well.

My football career was a different story. My mates and I had formed a team – Silverdale FC – just so we'd have an excuse to get together and have a drink on a Sunday.

It was only a park team and I was the goalkeeper. I basically used all my rugby skills, which didn't really work too well and wasn't appreciated by the opposition or the officials. I remember one referee describing my style of play as "absolutely mental". He probably had a point.

Things weren't going well at work either. I passed my apprenticeship, but along with all the other apprentices from my year, I was not kept on at Mobil.

I struggled to find work after that and ended up labouring for a while, working back in the same refinery where I'd been an apprentice. I was sweeping up and shovelling the mess I would have been making only a few months before. It was tough because the guys I was cleaning up after were also the people who had trained me to be an engineer.

Now I was just digging holes for a living and clearing up wax spillages but it was a way of earning money and I certainly didn't want to sign on.

It was also quite fun, although one embarrassing incident has always stayed with me. I was up a ladder taking out some roof joists and, in trying to secure the ladder, I managed to tie it to the joist I was removing.

When the joist fell, so did I and I crashed against the side of the wall on my way down. Fortunately my boss didn't see my pratfall. Unfortunately, my mate Dave Bond did, and has never let me forget it.

Despite that mishap, I stuck at labouring for a while before getting a couple of weeks' work as an engineer. But I was then out of work again for quite some time.

A six-week spell in one of the big shutdown companies followed. They were long days but they enabled me to save up some much-needed money.

My mate Gary Smith – who back then was a good Canvey Island lad complete with dreadlocks – was working at the same place. We would often speak about jacking it all in for a trip to Australia to the point where it became a bit of a running joke between us.

My latest car was another running joke. Being an Essex boy, all my friends had XR2s and XR3s. I don't know what was wrong with me but I didn't want one of those and I got myself a Sierra Ghia instead because it was comfortable.

That wasn't normal for a 19-year-old and everyone took the mickey. They'd even refuse to get in it, although that might have been more to do with my driving than the car itself.

The only thing I can say in its defence is that it had electric windows, which I thought were great but it was also that car I crashed twice. Around the same time as those accidents, my contract at the refinery came to an end. So did Gary's and our joke about going to Australia suddenly got more serious.

I was talking about my cousin Karen who was mucking around in Australia and having the time of her life. I said to Gary, "Why don't we go and do the same?"

We went home and told our parents, I went to London to pick up our visas and 10 days later we were on a flight halfway around the world.

Chapter 03

Don't worry, Mum, what could possibly go wrong?

Gary and I were both excited about heading out to Australia, but there was one slight problem before we'd even got on the plane.

Originally we wanted to take the standard backpackers' route and enjoy a few days' stopover in Thailand on the way. But when I told my mum about our plans she wasn't too keen for her 20-year-old, Essex boy son to go to Thailand at all.

She had seen some documentaries on TV and had this vision of drug traffickers slipping things into our luggage and us being harshly punished. That wasn't going to happen to her 'little angel', so she persuaded me that Singapore was a much better place to stop en route.

Mum said her brother, Peter, had been stationed in Singapore with the Navy many moons ago. It was apparently this wonderful place, really cheap as well, with lots to see and do.

It took quite a while for me to agree to this and it took even longer for me to persuade Gary, but I was helped by the fact that I was the one doing all the bookings. Gary eventually agreed so I was off to the travel agent to book the tickets and get my visa.

The day finally came to leave, only 10 days after the initial decision to go. As you can see a lot of thought went into our year away: get tickets; fly to Sydney; "Is Sydney top or bottom?", "Who cares?"; Meet Karen; go to pub. There, year planned.

I can still remember being at Heathrow with my parents and meeting up with Gary and his family. They were saying goodbye to their 20-year-old sons and would have no way of getting in touch with us for the next year so it must have been quite nerve-racking.

These days there are mobile phones, Facebook and Skype but this was 1993 –practically the dark ages – and it was all very different back then. Our families knew they had to rely on these two hapless Essex boys to remember to phone home or send the occasional letter.

We had our last meals together before Gary and I said our goodbyes. As we passed through customs it all started to feel very real.

The tickets we had were the cheapest we could get so our first stop was Paris, although we didn't get to see any of it – we just sat at Charles de Gaulle airport for about four hours before boarding the next flight. Finally we were on our way to Singapore.

I'm a bit more energetic than Gary so it made for an interesting flight. There were no television screens in the back of the seats back then, you either watched a rubbish film on a small screen 15 rows away down the plane, or you made your own entertainment.

Gary was happy to amuse himself by simply trying to get some sleep. I, on the other hand, amused myself by trying to keep him awake.

Before we knew it we had arrived in Singapore. The trip started on a huge high when we arrived at our hotel and found we were booked into an absolutely massive room – big enough for a game of football, as we quickly proved with some rolled-up socks. And there were three bathrooms – more than one each!

We were only there for three nights so we decided to make the most of it and start the trip in style, with a beer. But as we bought the first round we discovered Singapore was no longer the cheap paradise my mum had portrayed. At the time it was working out to be around £6 a pint so we ended up having a very dry first three days. Obviously this was not how we had planned to start our trip to Australia.

Mum has never admitted it but I bet she knew. To say we couldn't wait to get out of Singapore was an understatement.

On our arrival in Sydney we were met by my cousin, Karen, who had been out there for six months and was quite settled. She took us to a flat she shared with friends in Chatswood, just outside Sydney. The plan was that we would stay there for a while, until we found our feet and could set up something more permanent.

After three very dry nights in Singapore, we were both more than ready to sample some of Australia's famous beers. That first night I reckon we worked our way through most of the beers available.

On our return to the flat in the small hours I managed to knock over a vase and drop a bottle of aftershave in the bathroom. Obviously I blamed the jetlag, but it wasn't the best way to announce my arrival.

The second day did not go much better, so on day three we decided to take ourselves out of the way and go to the beach.

We headed to the nearest train station, about a quarter of a mile up the road, and asked for two tickets to the beach. We jumped on the train but an hour and a half later we were in the middle of the countryside starting to think something wasn't right – last time I looked, Sydney had a coastline. We decided to get off and jumped on a train heading back in the opposite direction.

An hour and a half later we were back where we started. Two stations after that we arrived at the beach we had spent the last three hours looking for.

That day finished with another huge night of drinking and, after just three nights, my cousin and her friends decided it might be a better idea for Gary and me to find a backpackers' hostel to stay in.

So off we went to the only place we really knew in Australia, Bondi Beach, where we found the perfect accommodation for us. We stayed there for a few weeks and met an amazing group of people.

It was a fantastic start to our year in Australia and we really felt young and free. We soon fitted in with a good group of friends and pretty much every day would follow the same pattern: we would wake up some time after noon and have some sandwiches from the local bakers for lunch. The first one to give in to the hunger had to go and get them. That was always me.

Then we would promise ourselves we wouldn't drink that night.

We would get some more food for dinner – basically two-minute noodles and whatever you could find to go with them. We'd then sit in the common room and the whole hostel would shut down at 6 o'clock when *The Simpsons* came on.

You could be on the phone to your parents, cooking your dinner or doing whatever, but whenever the call came that *The Simpsons* was starting you just stopped and headed to the television. There were about 60 of us staying there and we would all swarm into the common room.

The group I was with at the time would all then sit there until someone would suggest we went out for 'just one drink'. We'd all agree, get showered and changed, and head to a local pub called the Bondi Hotel.

The next thing we knew it was 4 o'clock in the morning, we were in King's Cross and we'd done it again.

All this drinking meant I soon started to run out of money. But my dad's uncle, John lives near Newcastle, about two hours north of Sydney, and luckily he said he could get us both some work, which was just what we needed.

John was working for the council at the time so we went off to the dairy farm where he lived with his wife, Krys. We stayed in a caravan on his land for the six weeks we were there. The farm was quite remote so we found it tough at first, but in the end we grew to love all the open space.

John – who I also called 'Uncle' – really looked after us. He did not suffer fools though, so we had to work hard and pull our weight around the house and farm.

At the time he had a beautiful, great big german shepherd dog called Bow, who unfortunately would always alert him whenever Gary and I stumbled back in at 3 o'clock in the morning.

Life there was very different from the hostel. We would be waking up at around half past five to go to work, rather than coming in at that time as we had been used to.

We did all kinds of things like laying down drainage and clearing land. But the job by far the best suited to me and Gary was when we were lollipop men doing traffic control. I thought we did it well, following one simple rule: see a young lady, turn the lollipop to stop.

I remember one particular job we had in Lake Macquarie, which was a stunning place. We were laying down concrete pavements in big sections but nearby was a local girls' school, which was just about to finish for the day.

Their bus stop was right next to where we had just laid the concrete, so my uncle told us all we had to do was keep the girls away from the fresh, new surface.

He then went away to carry on whatever he was doing, but when he came back the concrete was covered with all kinds of names, footprints and lovehearts. Gary and I just stood there with our arms in the air to demonstrate that two of us were powerless to stop 30 or 40 girls.

We stayed with John for about six weeks, but by then it was getting close to Christmas and we always knew we wanted to go back and spend that with our friends in Bondi.

The time at my uncle's had done us a few favours though. We'd really enjoyed living on the farm and had even managed to save some of the money we earned.

Getting accommodation back in Sydney proved difficult though. The hostel our friends were still staying in was full. We found ourselves staying at another hostel for a while, but obviously we didn't know anybody there and it was starting to look like Christmas was going to be a bit of a let down.

Luckily we weren't there long. Our mates in Bondi had persuaded the owners of their hostel to add another set of bunks to their room (if you could call it a room – 'hovel' would be a better description).

There were six of us in this one room and I dread to think what other nasties lived in there. There were bed bugs and the door regularly fell off its hinges. It was a pit and no parent would have dared go in there, but we were young and we didn't care.

Soon Gary and I got another job, this time working on the chair swings at a fairground in Circular Quay, right between Sydney Harbour Bridge and the Opera House. As jobs go it was not a bad way to earn a living. We must have been doing something right because the owner wanted us to travel with the fair. It may have been the Essex boy swagger, but we seemed to get the punters in.

Christmas 1993 was one of those days I will never forget. We spent it on Bondi Beach with a dustbin full of ice and beer. What more could a young lad want? We hadn't really thought about food but, luckily for us, others had and, as it was the season of goodwill, they were happy to share.

There was the most amazing atmosphere down on the beach. Brits often say they can't imagine Christmas day in the sun – it just isn't right. Trust me, it felt very right.

The beach was packed. People had fridges, sofas and anything you could think of with them. There were people having full Christmas dinners and it was just amazing to be a part of.

We had an absolute blast and that carried through to New Year's Eve when, unfortunately, the fairground operators expected us to work. They told us under no circumstances could we have the day off, so that was the end of that job. I had not travelled 12,500 miles to spend New Year's Eve working.

We decided to mark the passing of another year by going out in fancy dress. I was a Roman centurion and Gary was a prisoner. To say we had a fantastic evening would be an understatement.

It was half past six in the morning by the time we got back in and I had lost half of my costume. I was now only wearing a white tunic and basically looked like a cross-dresser walking the streets.

During my time in Bondi I did remember to call home occasionally. This would involve queuing up at the orange phones that anyone who was in Australia in the early 1990s will remember.

There was always a huge queue and everyone in it would have the same conversation with their parents: "Hi, Mum" or "Hi, Dad" and "I'm having a great time," before moving onto "I've tried to find work but there aren't any jobs, so please could you send me some money because I'm broke?" I made this call pretty much every month.

A few weeks after New Year, it was time to move up the coast so we headed off to Surfers Paradise for a few more days of partying before moving on to find work.

Next stop was Brisbane where we stayed at the Swagman's Rest, the hostel I would end up working for when I had the car crash. While there I got a job as an engineer and was due to start work on 10 February, the day after my 21st birthday.

Everyone at the hostel came out to celebrate with the aim of getting me very drunk, which of course they did. I only lasted about an hour and a half before I needed to be piled into a taxi. They couldn't actually get me from the taxi to the hostel so, as any good friends would, they left me in the doorway before going back out to enjoy the rest of their evening.

I was still in the doorway when they got back, so naturally they shaved off my hair, stripped me naked and tied me to a lamppost, where I stayed until they got bored of laughing at me. It certainly wasn't the best preparation for my new job.

I rolled up four hours late. I'd managed to find some clothes but still stank of booze and had a very severe skinhead haircut. I was sent straight home but at least they told me to come back the next day.

I worked there for about six weeks but it just didn't seem right. I could have been an engineer in the UK and the machine shop would have been about 30 degrees cooler. That's when I ended up working for the Swagman's Rest for the first time, as their van driver.

Basically my job was to meet people when they got off the buses that travelled up and down the coast. I would then try to talk the passengers into staying at the hostel.

When on night duty, one of the jobs was to drive your clients to the backpacker nights. My favourite was one called 'Monday Madness'. It was in the suburbs of Brisbane and all the backpackers from all the different hostels would go there.

There were drinking games and singing competitions. It was carnage. When I wasn't driving I was always in the boat race crew because I could drink a glass of beer very fast – an overlooked skill I feel, but one I've never put on my CV.

At the end of the night all the minibuses would turn up, and everyone would pile in. It was standard for the driver to pull up at their hostel only to find half his passengers had got on the wrong bus, so we would spend the rest of the night driving around Brisbane dropping people off.

Unfortunately Gary and my other friends left me in Brisbane, moving on up the coast after only a couple of weeks having decided the city was not for them. Gary ended up going home to Essex after only six months away.

But I stayed, working there for a couple of months before it was time to move on again. First stop was Fraser Island national park to do its famous three-day driving safari. Basically you get a Toyota Land Cruiser and a tent, and go off to discover the island.

It's pretty hairy with lots of young travellers cruising up and down the beach. The hostel I was with sent two cars of seven people each. Luckily for me the two groups stayed together as I had a lot more in common with the second group.

We drove round the island all day, visiting all the sites before putting our tents up and camping on the beach at night.

We stayed up until about 3 o'clock most nights, watching the stars and enjoying the freedom camping gave us. The first night, when I finally decided to go to bed, I couldn't find my sleeping bag so I had to sleep without. It was freezing cold and in the morning I had to sit in the car to warm myself up.

I put this all down to me being a bit drunk but exactly the same thing happened again the following night. Eventually one of the group, a guy called Darren, admitted to going into my tent every night and taking my sleeping bag to use as a pillow.

For some reason we stayed friends. So, with my sleeping bag well protected, we moved up the coast together to a place called Airlie Beach where we boarded a five-day sailing charter around the Whitsunday Islands. I fell in love with the place – Airlie Beach and the Whitsundays – and knew I had to find a way to stay there.

Luckily I managed to get a job driving the minibus at the backpackers' hostel I was staying at, Reef Oceania.

I had struck gold, the perfect job in the perfect place. I was totally carefree and would work three early shifts, three late and then have three days off. There were three of us doing it on a rota and, along with Darren, who had one of the other bus driver jobs, we all shared a cabin together – Room 205.

My role was to meet the clients off the buses and tout for business from my allocated booth. I was paid a weekly wage plus another dollar for every person I got who wasn't booked.

I was quite good at touting and persuading people to stay in our hostel. I would also recommend the best boat trips for people as well, which meant on my days off the boats would let me on free of charge. What a life.

It was here that I first learnt to scuba dive, and I quickly fell in love with the area's underwater paradise. I learned with a company called Barrier Reef Diving services and very quickly developed a special friendship with the owners, Bob and Kay, who would later play a key role in me becoming an instructor.

What made Airlie Beach so special was the group of people that came together there. We all worked there at the same time for about the same length of time and all became very close.

During this period my parents sent my brother Paul out to spend a month with me. It was the first time he had been away on his own at the tender age of 18 and I was now in charge of him. Oh dear.

At home, he had been spoilt with nice food and things being clean, but when he got to our log cabin it wasn't quite the same.

His first night was one to remember, although I doubt he can. We'd recently started something called the 'century club', which involved drinking 100 shot glasses of beer in 100 minutes so every minute you would have a shot. Soon all the other hostels were coming to join in and it became a regular thing.

When Paul arrived, it seemed only fitting to mark the occasion with a century club in his honour. In togas.

I think you can safely say he enjoyed his four weeks with us, so much so he returned a few years later to spend a year there himself.

The four months I spent in Airlie Beach were among the best in my life – partly because it was such a beautiful location, but mostly because of the friends I made. There were about 15 to 20 of us in a close group and we were never apart.

Sadly, this couldn't last forever. The terms of my ticket meant I had to complete the journey from Sydney to Cairns within my year in Australia, so I had to say goodbye to my friends and moved on with Launa, a Canadian girl I was going out with at the time.

The next stop for us was Townsville, followed by Magnetic Island. There Launa and I said our goodbyes, believing we would probably never see each other again, although we did have a brief reunion when she came to visit me in the hospital.

Once we separated I was off to Cairns for the last leg of my journey. For a sociable guy I always seemed to travel alone. In the past this had not been an issue, but now I was starting to miss my friends back in Airlie.

Once in Cairns I did a few touristy things – mainly drink-orientated – and started to think about the prospects of returning to the UK. This meant looking for my flight ticket home, which I'd buried deep in the bottom of my back-pack, partly hoping I would never need it.

This was about a week before the date of the flight I was booked on, but when I dug out the ticket I noticed it would expire a few days before that flight left. To make matters worse I still had to get from Cairns to Sydney to get the flight.

I suddenly realised what had happened – I had bought the ticket 10 days before I flew to Australia. I had been thinking I had a year from the date I had arrived, not the date I purchased the ticket.

I did have two days to try to get a flight but none were available before the ticket would expire. I explained my predicament to Air France but they were not too quick to offer the opportunity for me to get on the next flight, so I was now stranded in Australia with no way of getting home.

With this in mind, I did the only thing I could think of and made a phone call: "Dad, a funny thing, but I've missed my flight home."

Dad listened and then told me that this time I was on my own. I would have to get myself out of this one.

To give myself a bit of breathing space I went back to the Swagman's Rest in Brisbane. They had agreed to fund my ticket home if I worked for them for a short period of time, doing the tasks as before, driving the minibus and working in reception. I did this for a few weeks and was able to book my flight home.

But before I left, there was one final job, to drive up the coast as far as Airlie Beach, delivering our brochures to backpackers as we went.

The owner of the Swagman's Rest, a man we knew as JR, had bought an old car for us to use. He had other plans for it afterwards. I think he was hoping to hire it out to other backpackers.

Unfortunately this time I was not going to travel alone. The manager, Barry, would accompany me and I would have to listen to his endless stories.

So, on 9 October 1994 – a sunny Tuesday afternoon – we set off from Brisbane for Airlie Beach. First stop Noosa, then Hervey Bay, the gateway to Fraser Island, and so on. It was only once I got into the journey that Barry decided to tell me that he'd lost his licence. Great, now I would have to do all the driving too.

We found a quiet place to stop at night and got our heads down in the car before setting off again at sunrise.

I don't remember too much about that journey, it was pretty uneventful. About 40 minutes south of Sarina we stopped for a rest and then set off again. The next thing I remember was the ditch.

Chapter 04

Rehab the Jack Daniel's way

Going home would have been hard enough anyway. I'd had 12 months away from everyday life. Even before the accident, I wasn't looking forward to going back to Essex at the end of the year and having to slot back into the old routine.

I have a really big group of friends in Corringham and they were a huge help. Dave Bond, Steve Whittaker, Ritchie Buttling and Paul Greene were my core group of mates before I went away and they were there for me in a big way when I got back too.

As well as that Thurrock – my old rugby club – were very supportive and their physiotherapist at the time, Kevin Lidlow, started to treat me twice a week. He told me it was to strengthen my back and arm but I found out many years later they didn't really need treatment at all. Kevin was just keeping an eye on me to see how I was coping mentally.

I remember one time I was sitting outside his house at 1 o'clock in the morning, waiting to talk to him after he had been out all evening treating people, and he still had time for me. He was a rock for me during that period.

Other people also started to rally around, organising much-needed fund-raisers. Being a recent amputee, I needed loads of adapted equipment, from my car to everyday things like kitchen implements and none of it was cheap.

The mates I'd played football with organised a game involving everyone from the Corringham and Stanford-le-Hope area. The match was followed by a disco – any excuse to have a drink.

They asked me to play but it was still too soon after my accident so I was restricted to watching, although I was more than happy to join in with the drinking afterwards.

They managed to raise a lot of money and it was all the more special because the whole event had been organised by my friends.

The rugby club did a similar thing and arranged their own match for my benefit. Once again, it was too soon for me to have a run on the pitch but I think that match was the spark that got me back playing the game again.

The rugby club and football team were like another family to me and it meant so much that so many of my friends had gone to all this trouble to put events on for my benefit.

All this happened within the first six months after the accident, a period I refer to as my 'rehab the Jack Daniel's way'. I had acquired a taste for the whiskey while in Australia, which continued back in Essex. But my drinking was always about making sure I had some sort of social life rather than drowning my sorrows.

There used to be a health club near us called the Havencrest, which became a nightclub in the evening. That's where we would go when the pubs shut at 11 o'clock. I was always the first to go out and the last to go home. I had some great times.

Steve and I were always up to something. Once my mum found us eating dog biscuits at some stupid hour of the morning. Not only were we trying to decide which colour biscuit tasted the best – we were also trying to choose which dip it tasted best with: cheese and chive or Philadelphia.

On another occasion my dad caught us cooking steak and chips at 4 o'clock in the morning. We had the deep fat fryer going and the steak was under the grill. Gordon Ramsey would have been proud. Needless to say, Dad wasn't. He cut the plug off the fryer and banned our late night feasts, so it was back to the dog biscuits.

I think I was trying to forget what had happened in Australia and I guess I did drink a lot, but so do most 21-year-olds. My mum did have concerns but for me it was just about having fun. I must confess I did keep a bottle in the bedroom though, just for those occasions when Mum would ask, "Don't you think you've had enough?"

I would agree, take myself to bed and carry on drinking there.

By now, many of my close friends from Airlie Beach had also returned to the UK and we all stayed in close contact. We often met up, organising reunions in Devon or Somerset where we would hire a cottage for a week. Reliving my time in Airlie and creating new memories with the same people really helped me get through coming to terms with being an amputee.

But if I ever thought I had it tough, it must have been even harder for my family having to watch their active, independent son struggling to adjust to his new disability.

I didn't have a job so my days were very dull and boring. I wouldn't wake up until around 1 o'clock in the afternoon when I'd wander up to the town centre so I could buy a scratchcard and some ham rolls. I'd walk back home to eat my rolls and if I won anything on the scratchcard that was a good excuse to go back to the shop to spend my winnings on more scratchcards.

I didn't know what else to do and had no idea what I was going to do for work – I couldn't see anyone giving me a job as a mechanical engineer. I went for an assessment to see what careers might suit me and was told I would be a good car park attendant. That hardly filled me with optimism.

After that, my mum got me some part-time work as a shelf stacker in Boots, but that wasn't enough for me. The early starts meant I didn't last long there either.

I was pretty lost and didn't work at all for quite some time. It was also hard being back under my parents' roof because I had been living away on my own for a year with no rules. But suddenly Mum and Dad were asking where I had been every time I went out.

Part of my rehabilitation involved trips to the limb-fitting centre in Harold Wood. An occupational therapist, Libby, and prosthetist, Derek, were assigned to me and their first job was to bring my dreams of a bionic arm back to reality.

I soon found out that prosthetic limbs for an upper arm amputee were pretty basic. The first few visits were for stump castings and fittings. I don't know how I felt back then, but I think I detached myself from what was actually happening, the fact that my stump was being cast in plaster. For me it was just a process and gave me time out of the house.

Eventually I was fitted with my first mechanical arm, which was held in place by a strap across my other shoulder and controlled by rotating my shoulders forward.

I actually became very good at controlling the arm pretty quickly. Because it was my dominant arm I had lost I was stronger and had more control on that side. So, while I was training at the centre, I seemed to be getting on very well.

The problem came as soon as I got home because I'd put the arm in the wardrobe and forget about it until the next visit to Harold Wood. I don't know if I couldn't face wearing the arm or just didn't have the desire to use one. I never told Libby or Derek that, but I think they knew anyway.

I did wear it out in public once, down the pub with some friends. False hands are not very practical so, like most amputees, I had opted for a split hook. After my friends had conjured up every old joke they could think of and I'd attempted to carry a pint I quickly found myself looking for other uses. I noticed that the split hook would be excellent for pinching girls' bums, so it wasn't long before one of my mates' girlfriends had confiscated the hook and I was left with just the arm. That was the end of that game.

After that arm I was fitted with a second version before moving onto a state-of-the-art, battery-powered one, which I promised I would use. It's in my loft somewhere now. I've still never worn it.

I decided that I did not need a prosthetic arm for everyday tasks and, most importantly, didn't want to wear one for cosmetic reasons.

It was now time for me to consider driving again. As well as needing my independence I was a very nervous passenger. This had been made worse by my involvement in two minor prangs shortly after coming back, very soon after my accident. I had a hate/hate relationship with cars back then.

I'd been relying on my dad to drive me everywhere since the accident. He would even take me 50 or 60 miles so I could visit friends for a night out. He would then come back the next day to collect his hungover son. I bet he loved that, especially after having spent all week driving a lorry.

As a result, the money raised by my friends went towards a car. It was a Vauxhall Cavalier CDI, which I had fitted with a steering aid. It was a big step for me to have that independence back, but I don't know who was more pleased – Dad or me.

When you lose a limb it is not just about physical and mental recovery, there is a lot of adjustment as well. Things you do a thousand times a day and take for granted suddenly become very difficult. I had to relearn how to get dressed, tie my shoelaces, do my flies up and – scariest of all – teach myself to shave left-handed.

Of course there is a technique to deal with most of these problems. Alternatively, there is often a gizmo or gadget to help with everyday jobs, but I quickly decided that rather than carry a truckload of stuff just to make a sandwich, I would find techniques to cope.

The greatest tools you can have in learning these techniques are patience and a sense of humour. I had the sense of humour but lacked the patience. A combination of learning established techniques and inventing my own meant I was soon able to manage most things myself.

I also now had to learn to write as a lefty so I was given sheets of paper just like you get in primary school and was told to write out the letters of the alphabet over and over again. I gave this about two seconds of my life before I figured I could always learn to write again later. Most of my reports in school said my handwriting was atrocious anyway. I figured if I couldn't write properly with my right hand before, I'd get by without learning to do it with my left hand now.

I never really thought, "what if this hadn't happened?" or "why me?" but there was guilt attached to the accident. I felt particularly bad about the financial implications for my parents. I am lucky to come from a family where money is not important, but I knew the cost of the flight and subsequent stay in Australia would have finished my parents' life savings, and the legal expenses were already beginning to rack up.

Six months had now passed and I was ready to start rebuilding my life. My first priority was to get back to playing rugby. Well, training at least. I started to train twice a week, mainly just to get fit although I was also enjoying being part of the club again. Of course, having a beer after training was essential too. At least I could say I had earned the drink.

This was an important step – I felt like I belonged again – but it soon became apparent that just training wasn't enough for me and I wanted to get back to playing competitively. Hicker Reid was still the coach – and still formidable – so I went to speak to him.

He obviously had concerns about me returning to the game and asked if I had considered coaching or refereeing. My immediate response was, "I play on the wing, I don't have the foggiest about rules or tactics, I just let the other 14 do all the work while I score the tries and take the glory."

I just wanted to play again so the decision was made. But first I had to master the skills I needed as a one-handed player. I received so much support from the other players that I was able to get to a stage where playing was a possibility. One year after losing my arm, the day finally came. It was Thurrock against Gravesend and I was in the fourth team.

Gravesend were the first team Thurrock ever played so they had this anniversary game every year. A few of their players were slightly concerned about playing against me so Kevin the physio decided it would be a brilliant idea to take me into their dressing room. He told them if they didn't tackle me hard I would score tries, and that would not look good in front of the TV cameras. I wasn't sure whether or not to thank Kevin for that but yes, the Gravesend players did tackle me hard.

The Thurrock team was full of the players who had helped me with my training and they were all very special to me. My brother even came on to play too so it was great to have him share that moment. He hadn't played much rugby since I injured his knee in a match a few years earlier. The less said about that the better.

The game attracted a lot of media attention, I think because it was a feel-good story on a wet November afternoon. Local and national newspapers were there and Rugby Special, the old BBC rugby highlights show, came along.

Originally they planned to get a bit of footage and run a package the following week, but no one could have imagined how well the game would go. I scored a hat-trick of tries and put in some good tackles.

For the media it was now a rush to get the story out. Rugby Special ended up running a lengthy piece and the story featured in many national newspapers. It was even picked up in Australia, New Zealand and Canada.

But for me this was about rebuilding my life, and I am certain that game was the biggest and most important step on my road to recovery. From that moment I realised no matter what had happened to me, I could still do the things I loved.

Ironically my handling skills were probably better with just one arm. I felt I was expected to drop every pass so the pressure was off. I even caught the odd high ball, which surprised me more than the opposition.

I played for Thurrock week in, week out, thoroughly enjoying being part of a team again. I soon found out though that opposition players would go to desperate lengths to stop 'the one-armed winger'. I have a photo of me running down the wing being chased by five players – one third of the other team. For the record, I did score on that occasion.

Just as I was getting properly settled back into everyday life in Essex, I got the call to go back to Australia for a court case, where I would be accused of crossing the white line and causing an accident.

The costs were mounting, so Dad and I flew Airtours to save on the fare. The journey took six different flights and 36 hours, but it was cheap.

Knowing that losing the case would make it harder for me to claim compensation in the future, we put a lot into fighting the charge. On top of the flights and the legal fees we paid $800 for an engineer's report into the accident.

I wasn't happy with how the police had handled everything at the time of the crash. The other driver – a 74-year-old local farmer – had an 8ft bulldozer blade on his truck, which the police had completely ignored in their incident report. My engineer's report argued that this blade would probably affect the handling of his truck and was almost certainly what had caused the damage.

Unfortunately we submitted the report too late for it to be admitted as evidence. We should probably have realised then we were fighting a losing battle but, having flown into Brisbane to meet with our solicitors, Dad and I flew onto Mackay to face the charge.

Once inside the courtroom, for all the expense of my solicitor and barrister, the magistrate just didn't seem interested.

At further expense we'd flown Barry, my passenger, to Mackay to act as my witness. During the hearing the other driver admitted to carrying a bulldozer blade and that he had not come to my aid after the accident, instead just changing his tyres. The police also admitted they hadn't breathalysed him.

Despite all these admissions and evidence, the whole thing was practically over before it started. Just half an hour later, I was found guilty and sent from the courtroom with a $30 fine and costs to pay.

The result was a disaster, but we still had a few days left before we were due to fly back to England, so Dad and I headed up to Airlie Beach again to try to make the best of it.

Still smarting from the growing expense of the legal process we stayed in one of the hostels I knew from my previous times there. It was great to have a few nights out with old friends, although Dad mostly chose to stay in. My dad likes a drink, but I don't think he was ready for a 23-year-old's night out in Airlie.

Too soon, we had to fly back to Britain. Another 36-hour journey and we were home, vowing never to fly Airtours again.

Now I had to put the setback of the court case behind me and get back into the routine I'd established over the previous year. I threw myself back into my rugby and spent a lot of time with my friends, but I still had not found any work and needed to find a way of earning of a living.

Chapter 05

Don't worry, Mum, but I'm going back to Australia

Before the accident I had learned to scuba dive in Australia, and this was something I was keen to pick up again. I came across a charity called the Scuba Trust, which specialises in teaching people with disabilities to dive. Leon Golding, one of the founders of the charity, explained what they did, and told me all about the amazing holidays the Trust would go on.

At the time I didn't want to be too involved because I was trying to distance myself from anything that had the label 'disability' attached to it. I wasn't ready to accept my disability and was trying to live an able-bodied life, so at first I didn't pursue any training with them.

Then one day, out of the blue, my occupational therapist gave me a leaflet for the Winston Churchill Memorial Travelling Fellowship. I read it and found that every year the organisation sent 100 people abroad to study in various fields so they could bring their new knowledge and skills back to Britain when they returned.

There are different categories each year and this year one just happened to be sport. This got me thinking about scuba diving again, and I remembered with envy what an amazing job the instructors in Australia had, being able to embrace that underwater world every day and being able to introduce others to it. That and the fact that women seemed to pay a lot of attention to the male instructors gave me all the reasons I needed.

I put in an application saying I wanted to go back to Australia to train as a scuba-driving instructor in the hope I could teach people with disabilities to dive in the future

Amazingly to me, they went for it and I was offered a travelling fellowship. They usually last for a maximum of six weeks but I was allowed to extend mine to three months so I could gain experience as well as training.

I flew back to Airlie Beach (where else?) and was taken on by a couple called John and Penny who owned a diving company, Whitsunday magic.

I spent a three-month internship training as a dive master. This primarily involved taking divers on underwater tours, although there was also the less glamorous side, like washing kit and filling bottles.

After a while I qualified, so now it was time to decide whether I would sit the instructor course or not. To be honest I wasn't sure if I was even up to it so I went to see the course director, Tony Fonts, for some advice. I asked if he felt I could complete the instructor's course, but also, most importantly, did he feel it would be safe for me to manage up to eight trainee divers in my care?

He was confident I could and suggested I did the first part of t he course to see how it went, then we could decide if I wanted to carry on. So that was settled, I was about to sit my instructor's training course,

To help me concentrate I moved out of the backpackers' hostel I was staying in and away from its distractions. I moved in with a lovely couple I'd met on my first trip, 'Barrier Reef Bob' and Kay Kent. They used to own Barrier Reef Diving Services, the school where I had originally learned to dive.

Bob was famed for his barbecues, which always involved a hidden chili, and his mad inventions. The one that always made me laugh was his bungee belt. He had a tiny pool in his garden, too small to swim in, but Bob worked out that he could hold himself in place with the belt and swim on the spot to get his exercise.

Most importantly he taught me the art of the cuddle jumper. I was a hot-blooded bloke in his mid-twenties while he was in his late fifties or early sixties, but all the women would give him a cuddle and not me. Eventually he shared his secret: wear a cuddly jumper.

Kay was a lovely lady and had the job of controlling us because when together, Bob and I would always get up to mischief. They also had a Japanese student – Yasuyo – staying with them. We had some real laughs diving and me trying to teach her the art of drinking.

I had a great time during my stay and always referred to Bob and Kay as my Australian parents. I was devastated when Bob passed away in 2010.

The instructor course was an intense 10 days. Half of it was spent in the classroom, honing our teaching skills and learning how to structure a lesson. That side of it was fine as I was no different to the others on my course. It was doing the practical side, in the pool and open water, where I would struggle.

I was unable to demonstrate some of the skills to the students because my equipment wasn't standard and had actually been set up specifically for my use. As a result I had to learn to be very good at explaining everything so I could get the message across clearly.

I also had to prove I could be responsible for people in the water. The examiners needed to know that I could look after divers in my care.

One way to do this was by putting a hook on to my jacket with an adjustable line that I could attach to any diver in distress to pull them in. I hoped I would never need to use it.

As the course came to an end, all the skills started to fall into place and finally it was time for the exams, which took place over a very stressful two days.

First was the pool section, where we were given modules of the training course to teach so we could demonstrate our water skills. This was the big test for me as I had to show I had found a way of explaining rather than demonstrating.

I passed the first section so it was back to the classroom, where we all had to give a presentation. Unfortunately I made a small mistake in mine.

That meant I failed, but I was given a 'dog's life', which meant I had a second chance. I was given one hour to prepare a new presentation. All my classmates had already passed and they all gathered around to help. I think we all felt the stress. I'd thought if anything it would have been the pool where I might fall short, not the classroom. Thankfully I took full advantage of my dog's life and that left only the open water section the following day.

Unlike day one, there was no second chance there. If you made one mistake on day two, you failed.

As well as testing our skills, the examiners threw emergency scenarios at us where we needed to demonstrate a level of calm and react accordingly. In one of these emergencies I did get to use my emergency buddy line.

I passed and became a fully qualified PADI (Professional Association of Diving Instructors) Diving instructor. This was a huge step for me because, having overcome so much, I now had a trade. I was qualified and, as jobs go, diving instructor is pretty cool.

Even better, the Winston Churchill Travelling Fellowship extended my trip so that I could gain more experience. It was an amazing time. I worked for the dive school for a while teaching all aspects of diving from beginner upwards. I think I had found my passion in life.

I then moved onto another company, a day trip boat called Reef Express. We would take people to a beautiful beach called Whitehaven, then after lunch they would move onto a snorkel and dive site called Manta Ray Bay, although I never saw a manta ray there.

My job was to sell "try dives", a chance for people to sample scuba diving before committing to a full course. I would run through some practical skills on the beach then dive at the bay. This was tough work because I only got paid by how many people I could get to dive and 10 was the maximum I could take. I think the Essex boy swagger came in handy as I was now as much a salesman as diving instructor.

I will never forget one day I had my full quota of 10 divers, so it was looking to be a good day. I was just finishing the second group's training and we were about waist deep, just off the beach, when suddenly an American lady came running down the beach screaming, "Get out of the water, there's been a shark attack!"

I didn't know how bad it was at the time and, to be honest, my main concern was my 10 divers changing their minds and backing out.

So I told my now slightly pale looking divers that somebody had probably got a love bite from a reef shark, which is what I believed had happened. In hindsight, I should have realised it was a bit more serious when I saw the air ambulance landing on the beach.

When it was time to leave and our boat arrived to pick everyone up, I found out that it was the boat's hostess who had gone to aid of the poor guy being attacked. So when I flippantly asked if it was a love bite from a small reef shark, she just told me to look at her. She was absolutely covered in blood.

It turned out the man being attacked had been gutting fish and had thrown the guts of the fish back in to the sea when he was finished. He'd then jumped in to clean himself off – only to be confronted by a shark coming the other way. He did survive the attack though, albeit with serious cuts to his legs.

We moved off to the dive site, but as you can imagine, going scuba diving was suddenly not the most attractive proposition. To help change their minds I dived head first in to the sea with a knife in my mouth telling them I was off to kill the shark. It must have worked as I still managed to keep my 10 divers. A man's got to earn a living.

I ended up spending nine months in Australia as a diving instructor and loved every minute. To spend your days on the ocean is such a privilege and I had even cured one of my hang-ups without even trying. I didn't think twice about being the guy at the front of the boat, but suddenly I wasn't bothered at all by people staring at me.

Unfortunately, after the nine months it was time for me to pack up and head home to fulfil my promise to the trust and bring some knowledge back to the UK.

Ideally I wanted to carry on with the scuba diving back home, but I only like warm water and England is just too cold.

Once in the UK I went back to the Scuba Trust and started to work with them, teaching people with disabilities to dive. It was hugely rewarding to see people who may have difficulty on land enjoying the freedom of the water. It was also interesting as every diver came with a unique set of needs.

We would train the divers in England and then take them on one of the Scuba Trust holidays to the Red Sea, where they could complete their diving in a warmer, calmer climate.

Those trips were some of the best holidays I have ever had. You might expect a group of people with disabilities to be quiet and sedate, but you could not be more wrong.

I remember my first trips with them. In normal circumstances when you teach, the instructor would kneel on the floor with their students in a semi-circle around them. With the Scuba Trust it was more a case of where they fell they stayed, on their back, side or front. It looked more like a war zone.

I soon gained a reputation for teaching people with disabilities and became the main instructor at the trust. One thing that stood out early on was the difference in people with disabilities when they were in big groups. Normally disabled people are in the minority and are often quiet and reserved. But in a big group – up to 30 on some trips – they could relax and be themselves. This really helped me deal with any image issues I still had.

I did feel for the ground crew at the airports though. I know they are trained to handle people with disabilities, but the numbers we travelled with would stretch any organisation.

While very enjoyable, my work with the Scuba Trust was only on an ad hoc basis. I still needed to find a way to earn regular income and was still hopeful I could do it through scuba diving.

I was sitting in the garden with my mum at the start of the summer in 1997 when she brought out the newspaper and showed me a job ad. It read, "Window cleaner required. Must be a qualified scuba diving instructor. Please apply to the Great Yarmouth Sea-life Centre."

I had to call. They explained that they needed a qualified diver to go into the shark tank to carry out maintenance. There was also a display they scheduled four times a day, where they filled the auditorium for a talk about sharks. During the talk they needed a diver to enter the water and swim around the tank with the sharks – the perfect job for a guy with one arm.

They asked me to come up that day and to bring my dive kit. So I travelled the 110 miles to Great Yarmouth where I was met by the centre manager and a marine biologist called Mitch. They explained what they hoped to achieve and took me to see the sharks. I don't know what I expected, but 20 of them – the biggest being nine feet – was not it.

Next came the second blow, they told me the reason they wanted me to come up so quickly was that the directors where due in that day and they wanted to show them the shark display. So, for my interview, would I go in?

To say I was nervous would be an understatement. I sat on top of the tank and listened to the staff explaining that the sharks were not big scary man-eaters. I decided to confirm this with Mitch. He tried to put my mind at rest by explaining that the sharks are hand-fed every other day, so should not be hungry.

"OK," I said, "how do they react when you jump in?"

"I don't know, never been in there," was not the answer I was hoping for.

Before I had time to jump back in the car and head home to Essex, my cue to jump in came. Without a second thought I was in, remembering the only advice I had been given: "try to enter without a splash."

The sharks darted and my heart stopped for a moment, but it all soon settled down. I swam around the tank and the sharks generally did their best to avoid me. There were a few stomach-churning moments, but I held my nerve and was offered the job.

While working I would often come to the front of the tank and kneel down to wave to any children visiting. If ever one pointed to my missing arm, I would point to the largest of the sharks, a nine-foot nurse shark called Nobby. The joke got a mixed response, mostly they laughed, although I did reduce one poor boy to tears. I had to go and speak with him afterwards to put his mind at rest.

Overall, if the display was meant to prove that sharks are not scary man-eaters, I am not sure using an arm amputee was the best choice.

I really enjoyed my time there and even made it onto the local BBC news. But as the summer holiday season drew to a close and visitor numbers dwindled, my job came to an end.

However, the recently opened London Aquarium had heard about this one-armed shark diver and offered me an interview to work there. With much excitement I went to London to meet the team. I was going up in the world.

Before we got to the shark tank I was shown the other exhibit they wanted me to dive in – the conger eel display. The biologist also showed me the scar where he had almost lost a thumb to one of them.

If that wasn't enough, when we finally arrived at the shark tank, I noticed they were larger and scarier looking than the ones in Great Yarmouth. It suddenly dawned on me that shark display diver might not the best career choice after all and I declined the offer. I was once again looking for work.

Towards the end of 1997, the Winston Churchill Fellowship held its annual award ceremony. All 100 people who had been sent away that year gathered in London to be presented with a commemorative medallion.

All of us had written reports at the end of our trips, explaining what we had been up to and what we had learned along the way. Mine was particularly honest and focused more on the nights out I'd enjoyed than any of the diving I had done.

Completely unexpectedly my report won an award as the best of the year. I was stunned. That year, the Fellowship had funded scientists, nuclear physicists and other influential, academic types. Then there was me who just went to Australia and scuba dived for nine months.

My prize was a magnum of vintage champagne, which I put away under the stairs in my parents' house. I vowed I would only open it if I achieved something special in my life.

During my time with the Scuba Trust, Leon Golding had introduced me to a couple called Mike and Gail who were running a diving school in the Costa Brava. We had talked about the possibility of me working for them, but I had not heard anything back all summer. So I went back to Thurrock and started playing rugby again.

Ever since that first game a year after the accident, I would get regular phone calls from a guy called Peter Arnott, who was in charge of the amputee section of the British Paralympic athletics squad.

He had seen the footage from my rugby game and knew I had competed as an athlete in the past. His offer was simple. There were two years until the next Paralympic Games and his squad met every month in Sheffield. Would I like to come along and meet some of the athletes who had been to the Atlanta 1996 Games? And who knows, why not give athletics ago and try to make the squad myself?

Peter's nickname is 'The Ambulance Chaser', because of the way he hunts around for amputees. He was very persistent in calling me. About every six months it would be time for our little game. For a couple of years it would go the same way: "Have you changed your mind?" "No."

I saw the Paralympics as being associated with disabilities and I was still trying as hard as I could to distance myself from that word. Even while I was teaching divers with disabilities, I still saw myself as able-bodied.

My regular refusals didn't put Peter off though and the next time he rang I was at the house of a good friend of mine from the Rugby club, John Keefe. I was always around there, especially if he had just returned from one of his regular booze runs to France. I saw it as my duty to drink his wine and eat his cheese.

This particular time, quite close to Christmas, he was having a party and I had left my phone on the side. When it rang John's wife Sally picked it up and said it was Peter. I told her not to answer under any circumstances. Obviously she did the opposite and, seconds later, I was on the phone, listening to Peter making yet another offer for me to join his team.

I was at John's, so I had been drinking and my defences were obviously down. I finally relented and told him I would come along to the next training session and meet the amputee athletes.

But I was clear in my mind that I was only going so I could tell Peter I no longer had an interest in athletics and that he should leave me alone to play rugby.

One month later, on a cold weekend in January 1998, I drove up to Sheffield to see everyone train. Ironically I couldn't run myself because I had been injured playing rugby the week before. It had taken more than two years to get me there and when I finally did turn up, I couldn't run.

I met some of the squad and listened to their stories of competing as an international athlete and, most importantly, competing at the Paralympics. To my surprise I didn't feel like I was talking to disabled people, but dedicated, professional athletes.

After what I saw that weekend I wanted to be a part of the team and immediately decided to stop playing rugby.

Chapter 06
The beginning of my future

As soon as I got home from that training session I rejoined Thurrock Harriers – the club I had represented as a youngster. For some reason I didn't go back to my old distance of 800 or 1500 metres though, choosing to run the 400 metres instead.

I think I chose the 400 because I saw it as the toughest event. Being a rugby player, everyone respects 400-metre runners and, maybe, if I was going to admit I was a 'disabled' athlete, I had to compensate by being the most macho disabled athlete possible.

My old coach, Ken Smith, was still at the club training youngsters. All the while I was training for the 400 metres, he kept telling me I should go back to running 800.

Every time I saw Ken it was, "Dan, go back to the 800 and you'll do OK," or, "You're a much better 800-metre runner than you'll ever be a 400." In the long run of course, he was proved right.

In the early days I only trained three times a week, but by late spring I was ready for my first track race, at Mile End Stadium in East London.

It was an able-bodied league match and I was running the 400 metres for Thurrock. To everyone's surprise, especially mine, I was racing against another arm amputee from Peter's group, an athlete called John Pickup who had finished fourth in the Atlanta Paralympics and was representing Newbury.

He wanted to live up to his reputation and did so easily by winning the race, while I came home well back in last place.

Having crossed the finishing line, I collapsed to the floor. As I lay panting on the track, John calmly walked over to me. "That's how you run a 400 metres." he said, and walked off.

I didn't need any more motivation than that – John's instantly became the first scalp I was gunning for.

I ran a few more races for Thurrock in the early part of the season and gradually chipped away at John Pickup's advantage with each one, but as summer approached I had a call from Spain offering me the diving job on the Costa Brava.

The job was as an instructor, guiding divers through the underwater tunnels and caves around and under the Medas Islands. It was an opportunity I couldn't turn down. They agreed that I could work the early season but would be free to return home to represent Great Britain at that summer's World Championships, if I was selected.

It was tough trying to keep up my training while working and living in a holiday resort. I was far from the model of a dedicated athlete at this point.

When I first set out on this journey, I had been seduced by stories from the other athletes in Peter's squad, stories of triumph and excitement in far-flung, exotic places. I was really excited by the prospect of my new life as a jet-setting international athlete.

While in Spain I got the letter I had been waiting for: 'Congratulations Danny Crates, You have been selected to represent Great Britain in the 1998 World Championships. In Birmingham.'

The West Midlands was not exactly the location I had envisaged when I dreamed about the glorious athletics career I had before me, but it was a start and I certainly wasn't going to refuse my first international call-up. I flew back from Spain to prepare.

I was really excited at the prospect of representing Great Britain. To think how far I had come in only four years since the accident.

August soon approached and it was time for me to travel to Birmingham and join my first international athletics team. This would also be the first time that I would meet the other members and disability groups on the team: the wheelchair racers (including the legendary Tanni Grey-Thompson), the visually impaired athletes and the cerebral palsy contingent. All serious athletes, none were defined by those disabilities.

We stayed in the halls of residence at Birmingham University; our squad was on the 13th floor. That wasn't quite what I was expecting my introduction to international athletics to be like either. I'd heard about these plush luxury hotels, but ended up in an empty student's room overlooking Birmingham.

Despite the accommodation and the venue it was a great experience. I was enjoying being part of a team, with all the banter and the pranks it entailed. There was a lot of camaraderie, and everyone was there to support each other.

It was during the games that I first met an amazing athlete by the name of Oumar Basakoulba Kone. He was incredible over 400 and especially 800 metres. It wouldn't be long before I had him in my sights. Once I'd got John Pickup out of the way, Kone would be my next big target.

Life for a Paralympic athlete was very different back then. There was no funding and sponsorship was non-existent, so we had a much more basic kit allocation than we enjoy today. But to me that didn't matter – I had my first international vest.

Soon it was time to run. I didn't get as nervous then as I would later in my career, probably because there was much less pressure and lower expectations.

My parents had travelled up to Birmingham to watch, and this would become a standard, whenever and wherever I raced for Great Britain, they would invariably be there.

I finished fourth in my heat so was not an immediate qualifier for the final and had to wait for the other heats to see if I would sneak into the final as one of the fastest losers. To be honest I thought I was out, but I shaded it by 0.01 seconds. Of all people it was John Pickup that I had squeaked past. The narrow margin of my small victory didn't matter. I had beaten him.

The final was tough. To be honest I wasn't ready for that level of competition and was probably out of my league, but I held my own for a while and, after 300 metres, all eight runners were virtually in a line across the track. I actually found myself thinking I could win a medal, but within moments of allowing myself to think that, I suddenly found myself a good 15 metres behind all seven of the other athletes.

I finished the race ranked eighth in the world, but all that registered with me was that I had finished last. I vowed to do everything I could to make sure that never happened again.

The championships finished on a better note. I was also a member of the 4 x 400 metre relay team, which came away with a silver medal. I can still remember standing on the podium with the other three athletes – including John Pickup – celebrating with Union Jacks draped over our shoulders. Unfortunately that was the last time we ran an amputee 4 x 400 metres as all three of the other athletes retired and were not replaced.

After the championships, I went back to the Costa Brava and finished the summer season as a diving instructor, but I knew I had a decision to make: it was two years until the next Paralympics, in Sydney. If I was going to be a part of those games – and, more important, be successful there – I would have to put my career as a diving instructor on hold and properly commit to athletics.

After the World Championships I had been accepted on to the National Lottery's World Class Performance plan, so I did get some help, but I was a C-class athlete, the lowest level possible.

I was working as a fitness instructor and personal trainer at three different health clubs. My lack of funding meant I needed the income, but I was having to fit my training around some long hours.

There were no major championships in the 1999 season. I competed at the Dutch Open, but the season was mostly about run trying to improve my times. I was still training with Roy Howe's group at Thurrock Harriers.

During the winter I went to see the physio, Kevin Lidlow. While I was in the waiting room he introduced me to Donna Fraser, who he also treated. She was one of the UK's top 400-metre runners and was there with her coach, Ayo Falola.

Kevin asked Ayo if he could help me out at all but, at that point, I don't think it was a great proposition for Ayo. He already had Donna and Vicky Day on his books and my time wasn't really that good. I was still about two seconds off Donna's pace.

But as the 1999 season went on, my times started to improve. By the end of the year I had run 50.8 seconds, exactly the same as Donna's personal best at that time.

When I bumped into Ayo at the physio again in October that year, I had something to offer. He could see that if he helped me, I could help Donna. I was an athlete who could train full time. I wasn't as naturally quick as Donna but was physically stronger, so would be able to help pull her through the tougher sessions.

Ayo agreed to coach me. Donna Fraser and I would be training partners for the next nine years.

Chapter 07
Time to get serious

Training with Ayo didn't get off to the best of starts. I had spoken to him on the 'phone in the build-up to our first meeting, which was to be in Woodford Green.

But this was before satnav was invented and I got hopelessly lost. The frustrating thing was that I could actually see where I was supposed to be as I hurtled past it on the M11, but I just couldn't work out how to get there from the motorway.

Eventually I made it, but by then I was 45 minutes late and had missed the whole warm up. I didn't make the greatest of first impressions.

There was only a small group working with Ayo. Vicky and Donna were there and Catherine Murphy, another 400-metre runner, arrived shortly after I joined.

We went through a number of training sessions together as I quickly acclimatised to full-time training and all it entails.

Previously I had been training three days a week, combining that with a bit of work as a fitness instructor. But now it was five or six days a week and my training was now a bit more sophisticated than just running round a track. They introduced weights training, although the weights shack in Woodford Green was so cold that we often couldn't even hold the metal bars.

The sessions were really long and they usually took place in the evening. We would arrive at around 7 o'clock and spend 45 minutes warming up, if I was on time.

After that we would go through a wide range of drills, jumping over hurdles and breaking down the running technique to include high knees, back kicks and things like that.

A running session would often follow but during the winter that would be on grass rather than the track in order to save our legs. Whatever we were doing, Ayo regularly had us in pieces with the sheer ferocity of his sessions.

He had a reputation for being a task master and I could see how he had earned it. Circuits were a favourite of his but we often had to ask if he had ever tried the programmes he was making us go through himself because they frequently seemed physically impossible.

He trained us hard and I wouldn't get back to Corringham, where I was now living with my mate Ian Murphy, until around 10 o'clock at night. I would be shattered and would generally just flop on the couch, eat some food and doze off. As a 24-year-old bloke living on his own, I may not have had the healthy diet you expect of an athlete, but I was always too tired to do any proper cooking so would usually fall back on packet pasta with a bit of chicken thrown in.

Training was exhausting, but it was a real wake-up call and made me realise just what it would take to be an athlete. However tired I was, it was a great feeling having some direction and knowing I was working towards something.

Even then, it took me a while to get used to my new regime. The girls in the group were all incredibly focused athletes who had done nothing but run and train since the age of about 13. But I had came from an Essex-boy, rugby background and I wasn't quite as disciplined.

At the end of 1999, to mark the millennium, I booked a five-day break in Newquay with about 30 friends. We basically spent the whole time drinking, including a memorable New Year's Eve dressed in home-made superhero costumes.

I didn't do much running during the five days and came back a little the worse for wear. I hadn't realised the impact that sort of relapse could have, but Ayo told me in no uncertain terms. It took me four or five weeks to get back to anything approaching full fitness again.

I got quite a telling off as Ayo explained that I just couldn't have these five-day benders if I wanted to be an athlete. I did heed his advice, the next New Year I only went away for three days.

Ayo wanted to incorporate some warm weather training into my regime and my first experience of that came early in 2000 when we headed out to Lanzarote for 10 days. I think that was when I really fell in love with athletics.

All you do is train while you're away and the idea is that the better climate allows your body to move more freely and more quickly.

You're also quite removed from all of life's other little pressures and have nothing to worry about beyond the sport itself, which helps. You don't have to rush home because the builder is coming round or because you have to go out for someone's birthday. Instead you are purely focused on your training, which is a huge benefit.

The only down side to the training was Ayo's obsession with ice baths, which he was even keener for us to use during warm weather trips. I used to dread them, but Ayo insisted we use them after every training session.

They were supposed to be set at about eight degrees Celsius, but Ayo didn't think that was cold enough and would add more ice until he had got the temperature down to four or five degrees.

I'm convinced that men have more pain receptors than women because Donna and the other girls would hop in every day without a grumble, but I found the ice baths to be agony.

We did have access to some technology beyond the ice baths while we were at the camps and that was easier for me to get excited about. Electronic timing gates were used to time our splits, there were parachutes to make us run slower and bungee chords to make us run faster. You name it, they had it.

It was also here that Ayo first introduced me to a sports psychologist. I had always been suspicious of sports psychology, but my sessions with Britt were really useful. The thing about being a professional athlete is it is all-consuming, even when you're not actually running, thinking about competing consumes your every waking moment, especially as a major championships closes in.

Britt taught me some breathing exercises to relax me and, more importantly, trained me to think in the right way. Rather than just thinking about the race coming up, she encouraged me to visualise every aspect of it. I would picture the gun going off, how I would run the first bend, the time I would go through the first 100 metres in, what position I would be coming onto the back straight and so on, down to every last detail.

You had to visualise it all in a positive way too. It was no use picturing Oumar Kone beating me, I had to think about how I was going to beat him.

My problem was that I was never very good at concentrating. I would do my breathing, try to relax and put myself on the start line. The gun would go but before I'd even hit the first bend I would start thinking about lunch or an apple would pop into my head. As a result, I never really got to grips with it, although I did use some of the techniques through the rest of my career.

The toughest thing for me was the down time in between training. The girls I was with were more chilled out and were used to relaxing. They were happy to sit around and read, but I was this hyperactive 26-year-old who just wanted to kick a football around or throw a Frisbee.

They would all be sitting by the edge of the pool, trying to relax with their books and magazines while I'd be hitting them with the Frisbee, trying to get their attention.

In fact, the only occasions when I wasn't trying to get noticed were the times Vicky and I would sneak down to the chocolate machine every day when Ayo wasn't looking. We had to resort to this because Ayo would regularly search our bags to make sure we hadn't smuggled any chocolate into camp.

Our secret trips to buy chocolate happened even more during our next spell of warm weather training, in Irvine, California, just a few months later. There I became the first ever member of any of Ayo's training camps to put on weight while away training. To be honest I always ate everything in sight, and in America there was an awful lot of food in sight.

It was an amazing time but we trained very hard, even if the scales suggested otherwise.

We all stayed together in a big apartment, which Ayo had hired for us and we all chipped in to help pay for it. The girls had commercial sponsors who paid for a lot of their stuff while my lottery funding paid for most of my share, which was handy because the trips abroad meant I'd had to give up my work as a fitness instructor. I just didn't have enough time.

We were in California for eight weeks alongside the entire British Olympic athletics team. Names like Christian Malcolm, Linford Christie, Dwain Chambers and John Regis were all there and it was now them that I was trying to get to accept me as an athlete.

I never wanted them to look at me as 'just' a Paralympian. I wanted to make sure they could see I was working just as hard as they were. That motivation kept me going through some really tough training sessions and, again, it was the down time I found most difficult.

I was in an all-female training group and I found being away without male company hard, but the girls were great and they were teaching me how to become an athlete.

We did our best to keep ourselves entertained while we were abroad but everything we did had to be competitive. If we played crazy golf we all wanted to win and it was the same if we went on the go-karts.

Ayo had charts on the wall to keep track of all our targets and achievements, and alongside them he put up tables recording all our other competitions as well. We'd see who could lose the most weight, who could get changed quickest and, one time, who could even wee for the longest!

Because it was competitive, I would often cheat – especially at crazy golf, which I was never any good at. I would end up with minus points because I was always being caught out and penalised, but another time, my punishment was even worse.

Donna and I would often throw the shot over our heads as part of our training. This soon became a contest to see who could throw it furthest. She had never beaten me so we had a bet, whoever won would have to do a full training session in the other's kit. Unfortunately I chose the worst possible moment to lose for the first time and I had to squeeze in to Donna's crop top and knickers.

It was one of the most embarrassing things I've ever had to do and it wasn't long before all the other British athletes were lined up along the side of the track shouting, "Come on, Daniella."

Despite the entire British team watching me, nobody saw fit to tell me I had the crop top on back to front until the end of the session. There was no danger of me being made to do it again though as Ayo reminded us that, while he was up for a laugh, we had to remember we were there for serious training.

Weirdly I ran my fastest 500 metres ever in training that day. I guess I've always wondered if I should have carried on with the knickers.

It was while I was out in California that I met Denise Lewis and she had an immediate effect on my training schedule. If you ever wondered how she went on to win the heptathlon at the Sydney Olympics, it was entirely down to her attitude and her level of commitment proved infectious.

Donna and I were doing 300 sit-ups every training session but then Denise came along and said we had to do 500 instead, so that's what we started doing.

We did races out there too but it was strange. I was running 50 seconds for the 400 metres at the time. That meant if I went to an open event in the UK, there usually be four races and I'd generally be put into the second fastest field of the four. But, typically, everything in America was bigger and better than at home. They were seriously fast out there and the events would have eight races. And I would usually find myself in race eight.

During a break from training, a few of us went to the cinema to check out my big screen debut. The previous autumn I'd got a phone call from a friend of a friend who worked as an extra in films. He said that Ridley Scott was filming a big blockbuster called *Gladiator* that required extras to lose limbs in a battle scene.

He put me in touch with the agency, who told me they would want me to lose my arm. I thought, "Well, I've done it before. It can't be that hard to do it again."

I was called in and went to a massive film set in Aldershot along with about 20 other amputees. We were all made up with appropriate levels of blood and gore, before being put out onto the battlefield where we would play dead or wounded soldiers.

I was in one of the opening sequences, lying at the feet of Russell Crowe the star of the film, as he pulled a sword out of a tree. They shot this many times over three days. Finally they were happy and I could go home.

One of the other athletes who was out in America, Jennifer Stoute, had also appeared in the film although she actually had a brief speaking part, riding a chariot before having her head cut off. She had previously been one of the TV *Gladiators* – 'Rebel' –and was now trying to launch herself into acting.

So a few of us went to the cinema to watch the film and everyone saw Jennifer, but at the end they were all asking me, "So, which bit were you in then, Dan?"

I'd tell them, "Oh I was at the start."

In truth it was only many years later, when I had the DVD and was able to freeze individual frames and magnify the image to at least 10 times its original size that I ever managed to spot the back of my head in the bottom right hand corner of the screen. But I was definitely there.

I was still in America when I got the phone call telling me a date had been set to settle the court case for my claim about my accident. It was scheduled for May so I would have to leave the training base slightly earlier than everyone else.

It wasn't ideal. I knew I needed to work hard just to make sure I was selected for the Games in Sydney that summer. But I was forced to take a break from training and fly from America to Brisbane where I met my solicitors and barristers.

I got there about 10 days before the trial while my parents were still preparing to fly out. We'd agreed this was something we would do together and they really wanted to be there.

While they were in the air on their way to join me, both legal teams met to see if they could save fees and thrash it all out before going in to court.

My claim was for about $1.5million and we were hoping the liability would be split so we could get half. We could've been looking at $750,000. I remember walking into court that day thinking I could be a lot better off when I walked out, but unfortunately it didn't quite work out that way.

By the time I arrived, the two sides had already been chatting away. My solicitors called me in and told me the other legal team were now claiming my passenger, Barry, had changed his story from his initial statements. He was no longer a credible witness and I was told it would now be even harder for me to win the case.

Barry hadn't maliciously gone against me or anything – he'd just contradicted himself, which was typical of the oaf that he was. He was 40-something and still living in a backpackers' hostel. That probably tells you all you need to know about him.

However shambolic Barry was, I had been relying on him. Now he was out of the equation, I would be standing alone.

My legal team told me they would go ahead on my instruction but warned me that if I lost, I would be hit with a huge legal bill from the other side.

I could end up liable for seven years' worth of both sides' fees – around $100,000. I thought things over for a while and eventually decided not to go ahead with it. Maybe, looking back now, it was the wrong decision, but I was on my own – my parents were still on their way out – and I didn't want to risk hitting Mum and Dad financially again

They had been shelling out all the way through for various examinations, tests and reports so I just decided I didn't want to keep that going. I settled for $50,000.

That may sound like a lot, but I had been expecting 15 times as much. At the time it was less than £25,000 and I only got that because the insurance company said they felt obliged to do me some right. Once I'd paid my legal bills, I was left with pennies. The settlement didn't come near covering the money we had already laid out on flights back and forth to Australia, reports and expert analysis.

I don't really know how I felt about the settlement. It had taken seven years to get to that point and it had suddenly ended quite abruptly. My barristers waived some of their charges so I could still walk away with a little bit of cash, although it was nothing compared to what Mum and Dad had spent over the years.

My barrister did explain that I could have just left the country without paying the other side's costs, but that would mean I could never come back to Australia and with the Sydney Games that I had been working so hard towards just months away, that was never an option.

All in all, the end to the whole process was as disappointing as it was unexpected. My legal team certainly hadn't seen it coming. They took me for a drink to cheer me up.

I was out with one of the barristers, Dan Kelly, who was bit of a bulldog and reminded me of the barristers you see on television. We stayed out together until around 2 o'clock in the morning when he went home while I headed off for a pizza.

After that I was walking back to my backpackers' when a Maori Kiwi guy started to follow me. As I went down a dark road he caught up with me and asked for some money.

I told him today was really not the day to be asking me for cash and that if I'd had any money left, I would still be in the pub.

From nowhere, he punched me in the face and pulled my t-shirt over my head before hitting me a couple more times and taking my wallet, which only had $5 in anyway.

When my top came off he realised I only had one arm. He was suddenly riddled with guilt. Not only did he try to give me the $5 back, he started asking me to hit him to even things up.

There were probably times in the past when I would have happily settled things that way, but the way that day was going, I thought I was probably likely to miss him and punch the wall. I really had had enough so I just accepted the money back and walked away.

I'd already got to bed when I decided I should report it to the police in case he was going to do the same to somebody else. So I got dressed, went to the front of the hostel and flagged down a taxi to take me to the police station. The cab ride cost me $5 so I lost my money anyway.

I filled in all the police paperwork and was told to come back the next day so I could get pictures of my bruises taken for their records.

When I went back to the station I bumped into Dan, the barrister I had been out with the night before. He was in full court regalia on his way to another case. He spotted my black eye and asked what had happened. When I told him I'd been mugged I think it took him half an hour to stop laughing.

Mum and Dad had been in the air while all this happened. I'm not sure how they felt when they were suddenly told they probably hadn't needed to come anyway. We tried to make the trip worthwhile and went to Airlie Beach so we could spend some time as a family and have some fun.

My brother was in Australia again at this time, doing his own year abroad, so we hooked up and did some scuba diving. We all just tried to move on; there was no point dwelling on it any longer. What had happened made no difference to my life, it just meant I wasn't going to have a nice car.

At the same time, though I couldn't help looking back and thinking of all the things we could have done differently. I'm sure we made a mistake taking on the solicitor recommended by the hostel's boss. Six months after taking on our case he quit law to take a job selling encyclopaedias. You don't have to be a rocket scientist to work out something must have gone wrong.

He at least passed on my details to another solicitor, who then noticed the letter we'd written complaining about the police's handling of the accident had never been sent.

We should have found our own solicitor and should probably have got a UK-based solicitor as well, someone we could speak to regularly and who would help make sure nothing was being missed.

Ultimately I probably shouldn't have backed down at the end either but I just had to put it behind me and get on with life. That meant picking up my training again.

First, though, I had to spend a frustrating week resting to let my body recover from the journey. I had already ended up flying out for the court case at roughly the same time as my colleagues were coming back from America, so they were back into full training schedules while I was dividing my time between courtrooms, being mugged and Airlie Beach. Training had not been high on my list of priorities during my time in Australia.

When I did get back into training I had to start in the gym and spent another week there before resuming my full programme. By the time I was back running, I was four to six weeks behind everyone else in terms of my preparation.

Everyone else had come back really fit and fast after an intensive eight weeks in America and had started racing straight away, but my detour to Australia meant I had missed the first part of the UK track season. I would spend most of the year just trying to catch up – hardly ideal with the Paralympics fast approaching.

As soon as I could run again I just got my head down, ran some races and did what I could to prepare for Sydney, even though at this stage I still hadn't been selected.

The selection process for the Paralympics is far less straightforward than the Olympics. There are only about 30 places in the whole athletics squad up for grabs and you have to run the qualifying time set by the Games' organisers to even be considered.

For Sydney, the mark was set at 53 seconds for the 400 metres, but the British team realised 20 athletes in the world could run that and they only wanted to take athletes who could win medals, so they set their own, lower qualifying time. To be in with a chance, you had to be able to get round the track in 51 seconds.

Basically, you had to be one of the country's top 30 medal shouts and it was a nervous wait to find out if you were selected.

I couldn't be complacent, but I did manage to run the qualifying time, as I had the previous season too. I also knew the fact I was with Ayo would count in my favour – the selectors knew I was training with the elite and back then that wasn't the norm.

Finally, I got the phone call telling me I'd been selected for my first Paralympic Games. It was a huge boost, but I wasn't happy with the way my preparations were going. The games were getting nearer and I was still finding it hard to catch up on what I'd missed at the start of the season. I always seemed to be about a month behind my peer group.

It got really hard towards the end of the summer because the Sydney games were so late in the year. The Paralympics did not take place until late October with the Olympics just before. All the girls, who were further on than me and would have to race a month earlier, were starting to taper down and get ready for Sydney, but I was still two months from my race, training at heavy volume.

It then became difficult to even find meetings to run at. The UK track season had finished and all the international class, able-bodied athletes flew out to Sydney, leaving me in the UK with nobody to race against as I tried to complete my preparation.

Even Ayo had flown off to Australia to be with the rest of his training group as they prepared for the Olympics so I was at home, trying to train alone with no coach, just going through the routines that Ayo had set me.

Eventually I flew out to the Gold Coast for the holding camp, but as I flew out, Ayo was flying back. He had been out in Australia for a month to see the girls through the pre-camp and the Olympics. Staying out there for another six weeks to see me through to my race was too big an ask.

1+2) My defining moment!
       (Australia 1994).

1) School photo - paying attention as usual (middle row, fourth from the right).

2) Street party - Queen's Silver Jubilee, 1977.

3) Mum with her two little angels.

4) Showing off my medal haul.

5) Early days running at Thurrock (not quite the international athlete).

6) Saying goodbye at the airport. What could possibly go wrong?

7) Christmas day on Bondi beach, 1993.

1) *Rehab the Jack Daniel's way with Alison and Shaun, members of my Airlie Beach 'family'.*

2) *Window cleaner (Great Yarmouth Sea Life Centre).*

3) *One of my early trips to Egypt with the Scuba Trust.*

4) *The perfect job - lollipop man in Australia.*

5) *One week post-accident, with Launa.*

6) *The one-armed winger (I'm the one in black and white).*

7) *Made-up for my 'starring role' in the film Gladiator.*

1) *World Championships, 1998. 4 x 400m silver medalists.*

2) *Training in America, 2001.*

3) *Chilling with my training group in Mexico (Donna Fraser, Catherine Murphy and Montell Douglas).*

4) *When Donna said 'Lets have a bath together', I didn't think she meant the ice bath.*

5) *A lost bet (training in Donna's crop top and knickers).*

6) *Opening ceremony, Sydney 2000 with Tanni Grey-Thompson.*

1) *Just me and 110,000 people.*

2) *Men's 400m final, Sydney 2000.*

3) *Friends and family.*

Chapter 08
Sydney 2000

I arrived in Australia a couple of weeks before the Games began and a month before my actual race. The holding camp on the Gold Coast was the same one the Olympic athletes had been using a month earlier, so I had access to all the same facilities at the same resort.

The training camp was amazing – a five-star resort with great food and everything laid on for us. It was a step up from the Birmingham student halls and several steps up from the backpackers' hostel I'd stayed in on my last visit to the Gold Coast. I had fond memories of my previous visit there – well, not too many memories to be honest – but this time I was determined to forge some new ones.

Everyone at the training camp was apprehensive but there was plenty of banter as we went through our final preparations. The camp was the only chance we really had to have a bit of fun as a team and it was important we took the opportunity to relax because we all knew what was coming.

The team flew down to Sydney in several waves, staggered according to how early in the Games our individual events were, although everybody was installed in the athletes' village in time for the opening ceremony. After two weeks in the holding camp, it was my turn to fly down, three days before the Games began.

It was my first Paralympics, and the athletes' village was a big part of the excitement because I didn't know what to expect at all.

From the airport I was taken to the accreditation suite to be given my security pass, which I would have to wear round my neck at all times. Once I had the pass, there were several more security checks and then, finally, I was in the village.

Inside, I got my first view of how massive an Olympic athletes' village is. If you think that the Great Britain team alone has about 350 people including support staff, you'll get some idea of the size the place needed to be.

The team was loaded onto buses, which took us down to where we were staying, and given a room key each. Essentially the accommodation is just houses and flats with all the rooms converted to bedrooms but at your first Paralympics, everything about it seems really exciting.

I was out the back of a house in a portable cabin, which basically had two bedrooms divided by a toilet and shower room. You could say this was my first insight into caravanning.

All the beds had these branded Sydney duvets. As soon as I saw them, the Essex boy in me came out and I decided, "I'm going to have that."

When I did come to leave, I rammed the duvet in my bag and was feeling quite smug, until I walked out and found that everyone had them. The duvet had been intended as a souvenir for us all to keep. I was half tempted to take it back. It didn't seem as much fun now I knew I hadn't nicked it.

The cabin had no kitchen and what kitchens there were in the other accommodation only really consisted of a kettle and a microwave, if you were lucky. But there were food halls that stayed open 24 hours a day and catered for every nationality with Indian, Chinese, Mexican, Italian food all freely available. They even had a McDonalds in there. We tried to resist that, but the Americans and Africans and anyone who had finished competing didn't have any problem.

The food hall is the most amazing thing about the village. It is basically a huge marquee where about 3,000 people can sit at once, with all these different food-vending places where everything is free. Of course the British team were more than happy to queue, but while we were all forming a polite line, everyone else just piled in and helped themselves.

There were big vats with ice cream and chocolate in them and as much fruit as you could want. I would go there for breakfast, lunch, dinner and any snacks in between. And as well as the food hall there were little coffee bars scattered around and the village even had cinemas. The whole site is so big you can't even walk around it – there are buses to take you wherever you need to go.

I was just getting over the excitement of simply being in an athletes' village when the opening ceremony came along. It was during these games that I first got to know the legendary Tanni Grey-Thompson and we passed our days in the village just drinking coffee and moaning, which we were both quite good at.

It was Tanni's fourth games and she really took me under her wing. She taught me a lot about Paralympic sport and how to deal with the big competitions, including valuable advice on how to keep yourself occupied through the long periods of downtime – mostly by drinking coffee and moaning as it turned out.

The night before the opening ceremony, Tanni and I were both bored and started looking for mischief with a couple of others. We managed to get into the stadium itself and actually stood on the track while some of the opening ceremony rehearsals were going on. It was a real thrill, getting a sneak preview of this spectacular venue but it probably wasn't the best thing we could have done. Sydney was huge – with 110,000 seats it is the largest Olympic stadium ever built – and when a stadium is empty it tends to look even bigger than it is.

We stood there with our hearts racing and looked up to the heavens, to the seats right at the back, and just thought, "Oh, my God. This is massive." Although it has to be said, Tanni was probably less intimidated than the rest of us – she went on to win four golds at the Games.

The actual day of the opening ceremony was obviously exciting, but there were about 3,500 athletes who needed to be co-ordinated so every movement had to be planned right down to the last detail. Those countries who were appearing early in the ceremony were bussed down to the stadium first, but we were quite late in the line-up. As the day went on, more and more buses kept appearing in the village. Eventually every single street was lined with buses and we were told what bus to get and when.

Everyone was getting twitchy with anticipation so we all went for something to eat, got changed into our suits and took a few photos, the excitement mounting at every step until finally we could get on our bus and go to the stadium. When we got there, we were put in this huge line with all the other competing teams.

We inched forward towards the stadium for about two hours, following a route all the way round the Olympic Park and through the basketball stadium. There were even places to sit down along the way. It's a well-oiled machine and one by one, countries were added to the back of the line as other countries at the front reached the stadium, but gradually as we shuffled along, the apprehension and excitement started to dwindle and boredom kicked in.

Just as I was starting to get restless and was starting to look for mischief, we got to a point about two or three teams from the front of the line. I could now hear 110,000 people going crazy, and the noise was getting louder and louder. We got to the point where the team before us walked out and the British team's flag-bearer walked right up to the edge of the stadium, to the edge of the track. As we stood there we heard the announcement, 'Representing Great Britain and Northern Ireland...'

As I stepped out onto the track, this massive buzz hit me as I heard the crowd cheering, the stadium going mad and music playing as we walked around the track.

Weirdly, once we were out on the track, I forgot that there were millions of people around the world watching. I even forgot about the 110,000 in the stadium and found myself just larking about with my mates as I walked round. I stopped messing about occasionally to try to find Mum and Dad in the crowd. They had told me where they were going to be, but I didn't really stand a chance.

Once we had finished our lap, we sat down in some of the seats by the track along with the other teams. The host country is always the last team out and, of course, they got a massive reception. Once Australia had appeared, there was a bit more of a cultural display and then the highlight, Kylie Minogue singing 'Waltzing Matilda'.

As the flame was lit at the end of the ceremony, it hit me that the Games had started. Before it had felt like an exhibition or a party, but once they lit that flame, my heart started pumping faster and I began a mental countdown, working out the number of days to my race.

The athletes who were competing in the first day or two had to miss the opening ceremony, so once we were all back in the athletes' village, we went for some food and told them all about it before trying to get some sleep.

I spent the next week going through final preparations for my race, but found it quite difficult. My team-mates would be off to the stadium and coming back having won medals, or having failed to win them. It is hard watching all that when you haven't even competed yet, trying to control your nerves and not let it distract you. I would be heading off to the training track while my mates, whose competitions had already finished, were able to relax and enjoy being a spectator.

A week into the Games and three days before the heats started, I had my final training session, then a rest day, a warm-up day and suddenly it was race day. The heats are always scheduled for the mornings so there wasn't too much hanging around. Although I'd done my share of nervous waiting the night before when I was trying – and failing – to get some sleep.

I got through the warm-up OK, and then managed to get through the heats too, which was a huge relief, just knowing I would be in the final. As a performance athlete, heats are the most nerve-racking part of a competition because you are expected to get through them. Once you are through it is just a sense of 'job done'. But if you get knocked out in the heats, you know you're definitely not going to win a medal.

I phoned Ayo straight after the race to tell him I'd made the finals and then started preparing. I had the rest of the day to get through, which wasn't too bad because for most of it I just felt an overwhelming relief that I had made the final. But as the day wore on, the relief gave way to nervous apprehension.

I hardly managed to sleep again that night, and then got up knowing I had a whole nervous day ahead of me before the final in the evening. I was literally counting the minutes, thinking, "In nine hours' time, I could be a champion." Then, "In eight hours and 55 minutes, I could be a champion," all the way through the day.

On the day of any competition, every last detail is planned. The team gave me a form to fill out saying exactly what time I was doing everything. I had to let them know when I would be having breakfast, having a massage, warming up, eating lunch, napping, changing into my kit, leaving for the warm-up track, getting to the bus station, what bus I'd have to catch, and so on.

Members of the support team appeared to meet me at every point on the schedule. They knew what time I was supposed to be doing everything and would be there to tick off each stage of the preparation as I did it.

It's quite subtly done but is really useful because when you're nervous you can easily miss a key part of the preparation. But not having to think about anything didn't help take my mind off the race.

Eventually I got to the point where I had to go to the stadium and every athlete has their own ritual around getting ready. My tracksuit would be hanging up with the rest of my kit folded in the wardrobe. I would attach my number to my vest and fix new spikes and check they were tight before packing my kitbag. I would always get the feeling that I had forgotten something so I would regularly go through one or all of these steps over and over again. In the build-up to the Sydney final I must have unpacked my kitbag to check I had my spikes and vest in there at least 10 times only to find them in there and have to repack it again each time.

Finally I had eaten and showered. I put my kit on and knew there was nothing else I could do. For me putting on the Great Britain kit was always a poignant moment.

When I ran as a kid, we used to get AAA badges that would be sewn onto our tracksuits. There were certain times for each age group in each event and if you ran the time, you would earn one of these badges.

I was probably 10 or 11 years old and I found an old Union Jack badge that was left over from the Queen's Silver Jubilee in 1977. I asked my mum to sew it onto my tracksuit alongside my AAA badges.

Mum looked at me and said, "You don't just put a Union Jack on your tracksuit, you have to earn one."

I've always remembered that. And every time I put on a tracksuit with a Union Jack on it, it always hit home that this was something special.

Shutting the bedroom door on the way out, it occurred to me that my whole world could be a different place when I opened that door again. I was either going to be bouncing off the walls, having fulfilled all my expectations. Or I was going to come back having failed.

Having done it enough times, I now realise that when you open that door again nothing really changes – there's still the same mess on the floor that you left when you went out – but I could never stop myself thinking that.

I set off to meet the team manager who would escort me and we walked up to the bus station and caught the bus to the stadium. The competition can begin on the bus. If anyone else from your race is on there with you there is often a bit of eyeballing and other mind games.

We got to the stadium and went straight to the warm-up track, next door to the main stadium. I headed to the Great Britain marquee where all the masseurs, physios and doctors were waiting.

It was hard because I got there early. I didn't want to be late, but I arrived half an hour before I even needed to start warming up, so I had to kill some time.

While I was waiting and trying to stay focused, there were people coming back to the tent having finished their races. Some were in floods of tears having failed, while others came back jumping all over the place having won medals and wanting to tell me all about it. Some were due to race before me and were going through their routines – Tanni was one of these and she helped my concentration by throwing up in a bucket in the corner. Some just looked terrified while the throwers were getting themselves pumped up and looking ready to fight the world.

Through all this I was just thinking, "I wonder if I just fell asleep here, would anyone notice?"

Finally I could start my warm-up and that's when it all started to make sense again. I had done the same warm-up thousands of times – every time I trained and every time I had raced for years. It was so familiar I found it easy to drop into that mechanical process and not have to think any more. For the first time that day I felt truly comfortable.

I went into the call room to register and then out into the main stadium. As I stood on the track they told us to strip down to get ready to race, so I put my tracksuit in the box and walked up to the start line.

I can remember standing there and not feeling quite focused. The public address was announcing the runners for the final and they got to me: "In lane five, representing Great Britain and Northern Ireland, Danny Crates."

I saw myself on the big screen in the stadium and all I could think was, "My shorts look a little bit flary."

The race hadn't started and I knew I was struggling. They called us to the start line: "On your marks. Set."

The gun went and there was a double bang. Someone had false started. I remember walking back to the start line thinking, "that was lucky" because I knew my head was not in the right place at all. I was slapping myself on the face and legs as we came back to the line, trying to get myself in the right place to race. You know what it feels like when you are in the zone and I wasn't. I desperately wanted to be, but the whole event had got to me. I was struggling and I just couldn't make it happen.

Races are won and lost in the preparation, not on the track, and I knew I would have lost that race there, on the starting line. Grateful I was getting a second chance, I tried to get my head together and settled back into the blocks. The gun went again and this time we were clean away.

I went off too slowly in the first 200 metres – I realised that during the race. When I got to the 200-metre mark I was already down on a lot of the other athletes. I would really have to work for the last half of the race.

Coming off the bend and into the home straight I'd worked my way up to third but it was a real effort, and I was just fighting to try to get it back. I was still in third as I crossed the line.

It was my first major medal, I was third in the world, but I was absolutely devastated.

It was really hard. People around me were all happy and congratulating me, but I was distraught. I knew I'd messed the race up. There were 0.22 seconds between gold and bronze and I knew I had made more than a quarter of a second's worth of mistakes during the race. I should have gone under 50 seconds. I'd felt destined to break the 50 second barrier that season and the Paralympic final was where I thought I would do it, but I ran 50.39. It wasn't even a season's best – I had definitely underperformed.

The BBC commentary team of John Ridgeon, Stuart Storey and Paul Dickenson absolutely slated me for the way I had run. I still show the video of the race at public speaking engagements, and I always play the original commentary and try to make a joke of it, "Don't you just love commentators?"

Some people will always say they were out of order but I always tell them I see all their comments as positive. As a Paralympic athlete they expected more of me; it would have been patronising for them to take the line that I'd done well just to turn up. Their criticism actually showed that they had understood Paralympic sport. Above all, I knew that what they were saying was justified.

I had to go to meet my family and friends and go through all the motions of being happy and jovial. Mum and Dad were there and Paul was still in the middle of his year in Australia so he had come along too with his girlfriend Katie.

They were all obviously pleased, they'd seen me come third in my first major games – I had been close to fourth so they were delighted to see me leave with a medal at all. To them, I hadn't underperformed, but inside I still felt broken. My family thought I had won a bronze medal, but I felt like I had lost a gold.

My expectations were so high, being number one was all I was ever going to settle for.

I phoned Ayo after the race, as I always did when he couldn't be there in person. He always said he could tell how well or how badly I'd done before he'd even spoken to me, based on how quickly after the end of the race I phoned him. If I rang instantly, he knew I'd done well, but the longer I left it, the worse I had done. It took me an hour and a half to get round to calling him after that 400 metres final. Ayo knew that if I had won, or even if I had come third with a personal best, I would have rung him straight away at the end of the race. An hour and a half was the longest I had ever left it. He just picked up the phone and laughed.

It was the only thing to do really, he wasn't going to tell me off or anything. "You don't need to tell me, do you?" he said, "What went wrong?"

"I went off too slow," I told him.

"Oh well, it's done now."

And that was his philosophy. There was no point in him saying anything. He knew I was going to beat myself up enough.

As well as Mum, Dad, Paul and Katie; my girlfriend at the time; a load of mates from home; Uncle John and his wife, Krys; and my 'Australian parents' from Airlie Beach, Bob and Kay, had all come along too. I was still devastated to have lost the race, but having so many friends and family there to share my first Paralympic experience meant the world to me.

We all went out for a meal and had a couple of drinks. I actually ended up staying out all night. I couldn't face going back to the athletes' village so I stayed at the hotel with my family and friends.

I forced myself to go back to the village at 8 o'clock the next morning and managed to sneak back in. At that time, the powers that be were very strict with Paralympic athletes. They didn't seem to get that most of us were adults so they set a strict curfew at 10 o'clock every night. But a couple of other athletes who had finished competing had also been out for a drink the previous night and were caught coming back into the village just after midnight. They had been severely reprimanded by the team management, who even threatened to send them home.

A lot of the senior athletes were staying in the same house as me and when I got in they were all sitting round, discussing what had happened and what should be done. As I sat down with them they turned to me and asked me what I thought.

"I don't know," I replied, "I've just got in, what happened?" They all fell about.

After that, I had to get myself up for more preparation because I still had the 200 metres to come. Ayo had a belief that to be a really strong runner over any distance, you had to be able to run one event either side, so back then I would run the 200 metres as well. We were trying to work on my speed, but I could never seem to get it right over the shorter distance.

With all the disappointment still in me, I had to try to prepare myself for another race, and one that we knew I was never going to win. There were two rounds before the final for the 200 metres and I had been hoping to make the semi-finals, but I was knocked out in the first round of heats. I had underperformed again. I'm sure that was partly because I hadn't got over the 400 metres four days before.

The Games drew to a close and I tried to put my races behind me and make the most of being there. The closing ceremony was great fun, much less structured than the opening ceremony. We all went out for drinks afterwards and then, back in the village, all the teams had their own parties so we rocked up to a few. My brother and Katie also announced that they had got engaged that night, which at least gave me something to celebrate while I was out there and ended the trip on a high note.

It costs the teams money to keep you in the village so they were keen to ship us home as soon as possible after the event was over. The day after the closing ceremony and having been out celebrating at various parties until 3 or 4 o'clock in the morning, we were put on a bus at 6am and sent to the airport for a 24-hour flight home, which feels even longer when you haven't done well.

The whole team flew home together so we pretty much had a whole jumbo jet to ourselves. On the flight, all the gold medalists were upgraded to first class, which made me even more motivated to make sure I had a gold medal myself next time round.

Before we took off, the captain came over the speakers and said he had just fulfilled a lifetime dream as he was sitting there holding a gold medal. I remember thinking, "You think that's cool? You're flying a jumbo jet." But I realised there and then the power that those medals have and how big a deal it is to win one.

When we landed there was a lot of press for the medalists. I sloped off out of the back and was picked up from the airport and driven home. I was living with my girlfriend at the time and had only been back a day when I got a phone call telling me that Brenda, one of the founder members of the Scuba Trust, was fast losing her battle with cancer. So the day after I got back, I got in the car and drove from Leigh-on-Sea to Buckinghamshire to visit and show her my medal. At least that seemed to put a smile on her face. A couple of days later she passed away, so I was glad I'd had the chance to say goodbye.

Then it was just a case of putting my disappointment behind me and getting over what had happened in Sydney. I had a long break, but soon it was time to start preparing for the next four years.

Chapter 09

Four years to become a champion

I suffered a blow before I'd even had a chance to get back on the track. Finishing third at Sydney had cost me a substantial chunk of my funding as I was now classified as a C athlete. Back then there were no appeals and no flexibility to the process. Your level of funding was determined exclusively by where you finished in the key races, so 0.22 seconds was not just the difference between gold and bronze, it was also the difference between full funding and having to survive on the bare minimum.

I wasn't so well known back then and didn't have any private backers but I had only just met Victoria, who would later become my wife, and didn't have a mortgage or kids yet, so I was able to get by.

My funding was cut, but it was off the back of the Sydney Games, that I was first introduced to the world of motivational speaking. It was difficult at first to get bookings. I had 'only' won bronze and, in the world of Paralympic sport, it's only really the gold medalists who got recognised and remembered.

I did a few local events, mostly talking at schools as favours for friends and family. Through word of mouth, I was slowly getting asked to do more and more of these talks and it was something that I really enjoyed doing.

At that stage I wasn't getting paid and I soon realised that, as these schools were getting further and further away from home, all these favours were costing me money.

I had a chat with Tanni Grey-Thompson, who I knew was quite busy working as a speaker. She introduced me to Creating Excellence, the management company who arranged all her speaking engagements.

They were happy to speak to me about the possibility of becoming a professional speaker and they agreed to give me a go. I went on a training course to fine tune my skills and before long I had my first paid speaking event. The Women's Institute paid me £50 to speak at one of their lunches, with some lovely sandwiches thrown in too.

My speaking career took me all the way through my athletics career. As my reputation as a motivational speaker grew, so I became busier as more and more bookings came in.

Since I'd stopped working as a fitness instructor I had been looking for something to do to support my athletics. I was aware that any sporting career is short and can be cut even shorter if you are unlucky. I wanted a back-up plan. It was also important for me to have something to do outside of athletics so that running did not consume my every thought.

The speaking took off to such an extent that I was able to subsidise my athletics career – especially during the tougher times.

But immediately after Sydney, my speaking career had barely begun, so I needed to get my funding back. The only way I was going to do that was by achieving better results on the track. 2001 became a very important year for me, financially as much as psychologically. I needed to prove that I could compete over 400 metres.

First I had another New Year blowout. Having listened to Ayo telling me off for my five-day bender over the millennium the previous year, I restricted my festivities to just three days this time. Not surprisingly, Ayo still wasn't happy and told me if I really wanted to succeed, I was going to have to seriously curb my social life.

This time I listened. I knuckled down and made all the changes he asked of me. I felt I'd made a big change in just joining Ayo's training group. Now I was making lots of small changes that would all help to make me a better athlete. I stopped going out so much, rested a lot more, started thinking about my diet and so on. People talk about these things as 'sacrifices', but I just call them life choices. Once I had started to make them, I felt I was actually becoming an athlete rather than just training like one.

By the time the track season started, I was ready. The first major tournament would be an open European Championships in Assen, Holland. I was competing against the best in Europe but was expected to win – neither of the two guys who finished ahead of me in Sydney were there – so that brought its own pressure

I won with a personal best of 50.23 seconds, a time I never bettered. Most significantly, the time and the medal were enough to get my funding restored to A-level.

The world record at the time was about 49 seconds, and I knew I still had potential to get better and to reach that mark, but it was becoming apparent that the two athletes who had beaten me in Sydney – Australia's Heath Francis and the Brazilian Antonio Souza – were also moving on and getting better and better themselves.

I could see that those two were going to kick on further and become the best 400-metre runners there were. Sure enough, they did go on to smash that world record several times between them, building an intense rivalry that I would have to struggle to break.

Later in the season, Ayo got me to run an 800 metres at an open meeting in Watford, where I ran 1 minute, 58 seconds. We knew that was pretty quick for a first attempt at the distance – not many can go under two minutes – but when we checked, it was only a fraction of a second off the time that won gold in Sydney.

It dawned on us that, because I had been running the shorter distance, I had this speed and power that most 800-metre runners don't have. At the end of the season I sat down with Ayo and we started to contemplate me moving up to focus more on the 800.

When we came back for training in 2002, I was still predominantly a 400-metre runner, but we started to lengthen my training, introducing endurance elements, ready for that year's season. I planned to run the 400 and 800 metres at the World Championships in Lille in July. I had now dropped the 200 metres for good, accepting I was never going to be capable of winning medals at that distance.

I went for the 800 metres, but really I should only have been doing it if the 400 metres came first. The theory goes that you should always have your main event first, make sure you do well, then anything you can do afterwards off the back of it is a bonus.

But in this instance, the 800 metres came three days before the 400, so running it at all was a big decision. I could risk tiring myself out or getting injured before what I still considered my main event. The only saving grace was that both distances just featured a straight final and I wouldn't have to go through any heats.

My first major 800-metre race went pretty well for the first 780 metres. I was in second with 20 metres to go, behind Oumar Basakoulba Kone, the Ivorian world record-holder. I was really attacking and it was probably only my determination to be the best that cost me a medal. Rather than settle for silver, I gave everything too early trying to catch Kone and a couple of the other, more experienced athletes overtook me on the line.

I finished fourth, but had only been 0.11 seconds away from second and was feeling confident going into the 400 metres. I thought finishing fourth in my first international 800 metres was OK and I still viewed the 400 metres as my strongest event.

But I finished fourth again there. While I could see a fourth place finish in the 800 as a positive, the 400 metres was an event I expected to win. The two who had finished ahead of me in Sydney – Francis and Souza were now both streets ahead of me. The Brazilian won with a new world record of 49.04 seconds. Francis wasn't far behind in 50.02 and Kone took bronze in 50.08, a good third of a second ahead of me.

With those results, my funding all but disappeared again. I had spread myself too thinly across both disciplines and needed to focus on one. As it turned out, I would never run another international 400 metres again. I probably would have done, but it always transpired that the 400 came first in the schedules and, after Lille, the 800 metres was always going to be my priority.

The irony is that when I ran for Thurrock as a teenager, I used to be an 800 or 1500-metre runner. It was only the desire to look macho that drew me to the 400 metres when I had returned to athletics in my 20s.

Before I had a chance to properly compete over the longer distance I had a 30th birthday to get out of the way. For about a year leading up to turning 30, I had been suffering from coughing fits that would come up in the middle of training. Also, if I ever caught a cold or some other bug, it would take me about a month to shake it off. If I had a glass of wine or a beer, I would get very wheezy.

I never really acknowledged any of this or did anything about it. For my 30th, we had a big fancy dress party and there was a fair amount of alcohol involved, but the next morning I was really struggling to breathe. I was coughing so much it was making me sick. Victoria finally persuaded me to see an emergency doctor, who immediately diagnosed me with asthma.

UK athletics has a huge medical back-up so I went to see the doctor as soon as I was back with the team. He sent me off for some tests. It emerged that I had quite severe asthma, which at the time was diagnosed as stress-induced. That meant whenever my body was under any stress – through sport, illness or just drinking – it would bring out the asthma. Apparently my lung capacity was reduced by up to 30% during these bouts.

I was prescribed a Ventolin inhaler and steroids to try to control it, but it became gradually worse throughout my career. Eventually it was no longer classified as 'stress-induced' and was diagnosed as full-blown asthma. I've never had a full attack, but I still get these huge coughing fits that bring me to the point of sickness.

I have had to manage that throughout my career since. It is hardest when I catch a common cold. It still takes me a long time to recover but, being an athlete, I can't afford to take six weeks off while I recuperate. So I would have to train through it while making sure I was doing whatever I could to manage its impact.

It was just something else I would have to learn to cope with. I couldn't let the asthma distract me as I entered my first full season as an 800-metre runner.

In March 2003, a month after my 30th birthday, the IAAF World Indoor Championships in Birmingham – an able-bodied meeting – included the 800 metres as a demonstration event. The race would give me my first opportunity to judge whether going back to my middle-distance roots would prove to be the right decision.

A lot of the other athletes had never run on an indoor track before, but I had competed at a number of Grand Prix events in Birmingham and always loved running on the blue track there – it felt like a big Scalextric.

The rest of the field didn't know how to run on the short, bouncy circuit with its tight bends and steep banks so it was quite a strange race. I went to the front early, as I always did, and then tried to slow the pace, but nobody else would take it on. The race got slower and slower and slower and ended up being by far the slowest 800 metres I ever ran in my life. At 2 minutes, 12 seconds it was a full 12 seconds slower than the next slowest race of my career, but I had a gold medal – my first over the distance.

It wasn't long before I added another at the European Championships later that season in Assen, Holland.

During the year, I also became a member of the British Milers Club (BMC), which ran a series of able-bodied meetings that I had started taking part in during the season. Initially I was running as a guest, but to be guaranteed a place on the start line, I would have to become a member. The only way to achieve that was to run their qualifying time, which in those days was set at 1 minute, 56 seconds for 800-metre races.

I had been getting quicker, and had even claimed a few titles, but my personal best was still one second outside that.

Before one BMC meeting in Watford I asked if there could be any dispensation for me to become a member. When I got to the stadium I had a chat with the guy at the check-in desk and asked if he'd had a chance to think about me coming in as a member at all.

He told me I could race today, but that there were no rules to say I should get any leeway on the qualifying time just because I was a Paralympian.

I left him and went off to run the race. Afterwards I went back to speak to him again about becoming a member, about 15 minutes after our first conversation.

"I've just told you," he said, "you will need to run 1 minute, 56."

"I just did" I told him. I was now a member of the BMC and I would go on to do most of my 800-metre racing with the club.

2004 would be a Paralympic year and I saw it in by staying in on New Year's Eve for the first time in my adult life. You can see how far I had come.

The year began with a visit to Aphrodite Hills, the luxury golf complex in Cyprus that would later serve as our holding camp before the Athens Games. I spent two weeks there, doing a bit of warm weather training in the Cypriot national stadium as well as a few longer, harder runs around the hilly golf course that formed part of the resort.

The trip was also a chance to see the facilities we would have in the immediate build-up to that summer's games. I couldn't complain about the million pound villa set into a golf course that served as accommodation.

The forthcoming Paralympics dominated everything I did that season – it was all building up to September and the big event.

Two months before the Games, I broke the world record over 800 metres. I actually broke it twice, but the first time, on a windy night in Watford, remained unofficial.

I was at another BMC meeting in terrible conditions. There was practically nobody around but I ran 1 minute, 54.7 seconds. Victoria was away at her parents that night so I celebrated my achievement with a cup of tea, a bar of chocolate and my dog, Kitty, for company.

Because there was no doping control at the Watford meeting, the record could not be ratified and made official. As it turned out, I broke it again weeks later, going even quicker at the British Athletics Championship in the City of Manchester stadium. This was another able-bodied event, which served as the Olympic team trials.

There was a good crowd, and my family was there, but the conditions were terrible. It was wet and windy, but I managed to finish sixth in a time of 1 minute, 53.2 seconds.

My qualification for the Paralympic team was then a formality. As long as I didn't get injured I would be going to Athens and I would be going as world record holder. Everything was coming together.

Chapter 10
Athens 2004

2004 was always going to be the biggest year of my career, but now my profile was higher than ever. Going to Athens as world record holder meant I had lots of media coverage in the build-up. It became clear that I had become the man to beat. I could feel the pressure increasing.

Ayo flew out to Athens with Donna a few weeks before I needed to go myself. I took the opportunity to go to Basildon Athletics Club, where I joined Eamonn Martin's training group. He was familiar with the demands of top level international athletics having won the London Marathon in 1993 – the last British winner of the event – and a Commonwealth gold over 10,000 metres in 1990. His group really helped me in my preparations for Athens and kept me going as I went through all the routines that Ayo had set for me.

Finally I could fly out myself and I arrived back in Cyprus, at Aphrodite Hills, two weeks before the Games. As with Sydney, there was a lot of inevitable anxiety around the camp, but it was important to try to relax and not get too worried about what was coming.

I was training with the rest of the endurance runners and we formed a really good team. It had taken a while for a lot of them to accept me.

Because I had come up from the 400 metres, they always viewed me more as a sprinter rather than one of them.

We had regular squad weekends at Loughborough University in the two years leading up to the Games, where I gradually got into their way of life, getting up at 6 o'clock on a Sunday morning to join them for a run. For a track athlete, even being out of bed at that time was unheard of and I didn't take to it straight away.

The other runners used to find it hilarious that, as they were running up this muddy country lane, I'd be getting further and further behind and all they could hear was this swearing behind them, gradually getting quieter. After half an hour running in one direction, they would turn around to head back to the base and the swearing would start getting louder and louder again until they passed me coming the other way.

Over time I got closer and closer to them until finally I was able to pretty much stay with them for an hour's run. By the time we got to that holding camp, I had earned their respect and we gelled really well as a team.

From Cyprus we headed on to the athletes' village. I didn't enjoy the village in Athens as much as I had Sydney, maybe because it was my second Games and the novelty had worn off. At the first Games, everything was exciting, but for me, now, running was more about doing the business and winning medals rather than just enjoying myself.

It wasn't all hard work though. I was sharing a room with Steffan Hughes, a guide runner for Tracey Hinton, one of the visually impaired athletes. He was a young lad and we got on really well.

Another of the athletes in our apartment was a visually impaired marathon runner called Paul Pearce. He was in his 40s but it was his first Games and he was just one of those really nice guys who took an interest in absolutely everybody.

He made more friends in his first few days in Athens than I had in six years of competitive running. I did get a little caught up in his enthusiasm, and allowed myself to get a bit excited as we hung our flags out of our windows and decorated our apartment in red, white and blue.

The opening ceremony was just as good as in Sydney and I continued my preparations as the first few days of competition began. My event was very late in the tournament so I saw a lot of my team-mates compete while I was waiting for my real action to begin.

As it turned out, I was the last of the British endurance athletes to compete. One by one, all of the team-mates running before me failed to win medals. Knowing that I was the last hope for a medal in that group doubled the pressure I felt, although I was probably putting enough pressure on myself just with my personal desire to win.

My heat was at 9 o'clock on a Friday morning, the first race on the track. I would need to be up at 5 o'clock but, feeling all the pressure of the heats again, I didn't really sleep anyway. Having got up and had breakfast, I was at the warm-up track by half past seven.

I knew my family were coming, and quite a few mates from home had said they would be there too, but I wasn't sure how many were definitely going to be able to make it. I remember walking out into the stadium 10 minutes before my heat was due to start. Because it was so early, the whole place was deserted, there was nobody in there except for one corner by the finish line where all I could see were Union Jacks.

All my family and mates who had said they would come were there, but there was a load of other people too, people I had no idea were coming. I couldn't look at them. I thought I would get too emotional and I knew I had to focus on my race.

I know a lot of athletes who don't like to have friends and family in the stadium because of the extra pressure it brings. If all your mates have spent all that money just to fly out and watch you compete, you don't want to have to explain to them that you stuffed your heat and won't even be in the final that they've bought tickets for. But I always wanted to share whatever I achieved. Even if I couldn't look at them, I was delighted they were there. However much extra pressure them being there brought, it also made winning so much more special.

I won the heat quite comfortably and shot round to see everyone. We had a quick chat but I knew I couldn't stay long. The final was the next day and I needed to stick to my programme. That meant going back to the village for food, rest, a massage and so on.

I had not been back in the village long and was walking through the British area when I heard our Chef de Mission say, "Your Highness, I'd like to introduce you to Danny Crates."

A member of the royal family was standing there and I chatted to them for about as long as I had my family and friends in the stadium. But I was so wrapped up in thinking about the final that I can't even remember which royal it was. It probably didn't even register at the time. As soon as I left them it was back to preparing for the final.

It was about midday when I got back to the village, leaving me with a lot of time to kill. I had a shower, packed my kitbag for the next day and tried to get some sleep, but I was too wired. In the end I just found some friends and tried to chill out a bit, had some lunch and a bit of dinner. Eventually I had got through the day.

Before I could even try to get some sleep though, on the Friday night, the team managers told me they were struggling to get Ayo a security pass so he would not have access to the warm-up track before the final. It felt like the end of the world. He had flown out just for my heats and final and, as an athlete, the one person you need at the track is your coach. I phoned Ayo up, almost in tears, to tell him.

Looking back, it was probably never going to be an issue, they were bound to find him a pass from somewhere and get him in, but when you are as nervous as I was, everything is heightened – I remember kicking off in Sydney because they couldn't find me any sprint leggings for the final. Every issue seems so much worse than it is and I panicked. But Ayo just said, "Don't worry, I'll be there."

That didn't really put my mind at rest but there was nothing I could do so I headed back to my room.

As I lay in bed, the start list for my final was posted under the door. Obviously I knew who I would be racing against, and knew I would be in lane four or five as the fastest qualifier, but seeing the names printed on a sheet somehow made it all more real.

The day of the final was quite strange. The race was not until 7 o'clock in the evening so the day would have to be filled with more waiting and hanging around. It might have been the longest day of my life.

Again, the whole day was planned. We'd actually been going through the same routine on the days leading up to the final too. We'd end each day with a training session at 7 o'clock, the time the final was due to start, to make sure my body was used to running at that time.

I knew exactly what time I would have breakfast, sleep, and so on. Now I just had to kill the time in the gaps in between.

Every athlete deals with the pressure differently, but I always became quite reclusive and would lock myself away to watch videos and DVDs. On the day of the final, I actually watched *Chariots of Fire*, I guess I was looking for a bit of inspiration.

I ate at about 4 o'clock: plain, chicken, plain rice and vegetables from the food hall. That was about all I could stomach at the time, I had been so nervous in the build-up. I remember waking up on the Saturday one week before the day of the final and thinking, this time next week I could be winning a gold medal. From that moment on, I never stopped thinking about the race. I struggled to eat, I struggled to sleep, I even struggled to hold a conversation. But having got that last meal down, I finally reached the point where I could begin my final preparations.

I had a shower and started the same routine I had been through a thousand times before. I put my race shorts on, tried the vest on, pinned on my numbers and checked my bag for the 20th time to make sure I had my spikes. I put my jacket on and walked out the door. I had that feeling again, that when I came back through that door everything could be different.

I got the bus at the allocated time, signing in along the way, and put my headphones on as I headed to the warm-up track. I listened to smooth jazz or classical music, anything that would calm me down and stop my heart from racing.

As promised, Ayo was at the track waiting for me. To this day, whenever I ask him how he got past security, he just smiles. I probably don't want to know. All that matters is he promised he would be there. And he was.

I got into the Great Britain marquee about two hours before the start of the race, laid down under a pile of coats, pulled the coats all over me and just listened to some more music trying to shut off from everything around me. 'Anxiety' by the Black-Eyed Peas would always be the last song I listened to before warming up. It's all about not fearing your enemies and it put me in the right frame of mind to race.

As an athlete, I tried to avoid too many pre-race rituals and superstitions. It can mess with your head if you miss a part of whatever routine you are supposed to follow. But I couldn't help having a few.

I always listened to Anxiety and I always carried my 'lucky dolphin' when I raced. Admittedly I was on my third lucky dolphin by the time of the Athens Games, having lost the previous two. That probably tells you all you need to know.

An hour and 20 minutes before the gun was due to go, I emerged from the coats to begin my warm-up. Again, I relaxed as I fell into the familiar routine that I had been through so many times before.

Before any big race Ayo would give his athletes a chat. Four weeks before he'd been at the Olympics with Donna Fraser, Catherine Murphy and Jo Fenn. Now it was my turn.

He said, "Come on, Dan, let's walk and talk."

I was expecting some big, gladiatorial speech that would drive me on to victory. We started walking round the track and he said, "Dan."

I looked at him, "Ayo."

"You know what to do."

And that was it. That was his speech. I stopped in my tracks and looked at him and thought, "You're right, I do know what to do."

Ayo knew exactly what to say to me at that moment and left me feeling amazing. I'm sure he said something completely different to the girls four weeks earlier, but this was my time. I was in the best shape of my life and there was no more I could have done.

I started my warm-up, which was strange because all the other athletes who I would be racing against were at the track too. I was keeping an eye on what they were doing, but still trying to keep some concentration and focus on my own warm-up. I tried to look supremely confident whenever I caught them looking at me, but inside I was in pieces.

I finished my warm-up, put my spikes on for the first time and did some strides, keeping my movement light. Then the spikes came off and I put my trainers back on.

Over the public address came the announcement, "Men's T46 800-metre final, please go to call room one."

The call room is basically a big tent, but it's right next door to the stadium and you can hear everything that's going on inside. That close to a big race, my senses came alive and I could feel the noise of the crowd.

I handed in my accreditation on the way in. That was as far as Ayo was allowed to come so he wished me luck and headed for his seat in the stands.

The officials put us all in a tiny pen, which can't have been more than 12 foot square. In this pen were eight chairs and several officials.

I was sitting there with the seven other athletes from the final for several minutes, but it felt like an age as the mind games kicked in. The African athletes would all look at me, talk to each other in broken French and then laugh.

I didn't go really in for psychological battles myself and just spent the time trying to be polite, wishing them luck while trying to focus on what I had to do.

The officials checked our kit, made sure we had the proper vest and that our numbers were pinned on correctly. Then they rummaged through our bags making sure we didn't have mobile phones, mp3 players, cameras or anything like that, confiscating anything beyond our basic kit until the end of the race.

Finally, one of the officials said, "OK, guys, are you ready?"

This was 30 minutes before the gun would go, but in Athens, it was a long walk underground from that pen into the stadium. We were all led through this tunnel system, slowly strolling towards the start line, winding our way through the bowels of the stadium.

Just as we were about to step out into the main arena we turned off and were put into another pen, underneath the seating area. Again we all sat, eying each other, knowing we now only had 20 minutes before we would be eying each other on the track.

The officials came round, told us our lane draw again and fitted our numbers to our legs. I was still trying to look cool in front of my rivals, but I remember struggling to stop my hands shaking enough to peel the sticky backing off the two number fours so I could attach them to my thighs.

We weren't in that pen for more than 15 minutes, but that time featured several trips to the toilet. At this stage, I was not allowed to go anywhere on my own, so each time I had to put my hand up and ask one of the officials to come with me. And each time he would wait outside, and be there to escort me back to the pen again after I finished.

We were allowed out onto a short bit of track underneath the main stadium, where we could do a few strides. It wasn't much, but it got me away from the intensity of the pen.

Finally the call came for us to go into the stadium proper. I picked my bag up and they walked us as far as the edge of the track. We stood there in lane order, watching the race before us unfold, waiting for it to finish so we could get out there ourselves.

Once the track was clear they walked us down the home straight, the stretch of track where the 100 metres was run, towards the start line. While the stadium had been all but empty for my heat the final was on a Saturday night so there were about 35,000 people in there.

I was trying to stay focused but my mind was buzzing and I kept hearing the noise of the crowd and shouts from within that noise, "Go on, Danny, go on, son."

I allowed myself a small smile, but I still couldn't look at where my friends and family were.

We were called to our lanes so I walked out, dropped my bag in the kit bin at the back of my lane and set off to do a few more strides around the bend to do what I could to loosen up.

About five minutes before the starting gun we were told to strip down, so I took off my tracksuit, leggings and t-shirt and stood there in my race kit.

They took the tracksuit away and then all I could do was wait for the official start time. There was a square box in each lane with the lane number on it, so I just sat down on mine and waited to race.

I ran through the race in my head a few times and stood up as the stadium PA announced me to the crowd, "In Lane four, representing Great Britain and Northern Ireland, is Danny Crates."

Finally we were at the point I had been waiting four years for and we could all line up to start the race. I actually felt really tired at this stage,

I had used up so much nervous energy in the hours and days leading up to the race. As we stood waiting for the gun I was yawning.

For the 800 metres it's just, "On your marks – Bang!" And off you go, you're away, instantly into the race.

My plan was to get near the front as early as possible without actually leading. From the gun I went straight to the inside lane. Soon Oumar Kone was on my shoulder, running alongside me. We ran side by side at the front of the pack for the first 200 metres or so.

I knew I was the fastest sprinter in the field, so I slowed the pace as much as I could, knowing that would leave me to finish faster. We went through the bell in 57 seconds, about a second slower than I had planned. That was good – it meant I would have a little more in reserve for the finish.

Wherever I was racing, as soon as I heard the bell I would say to myself, "wake up." It was a trigger in my mind. It's natural to slow down when running round a bend, so that little wake-up call always pushed me to make sure I put a little extra effort in to maintain my speed.

Luckily nobody went for it at the bell so I could maintain the pace I wanted, controlling the race until we had just 200 metres to go. Again I was just trying to maintain my speed round the final bend. By this stage I had moved a little ahead.

With 150 metres to go, the Algerian Samir Nouioua attacked really hard and came up on my shoulder from nowhere. Having dictated the race to that point, I still had my fifth gear left. I kicked in, digging deep to push down the home straight.

With about 80 metres to go, I had a clear lead of three or four metres. It might sound odd, but that is a really strange place to be. I was so close to achieving everything I had dreamed of and planned for but I didn't have it yet. I was just wishing and praying for that finish line to arrive, but it seemed to take forever.

I could hear Nouioua behind me, it felt like he was coming strong but really I had no idea whether he was coming quickly or fading. I wasn't going to slow down to check.

I could hear the crowd going mad, so I knew he was close, but I still had no idea how close. All I could do was keep kicking and I knew that finish line would have to come at some point.

Eventually it did. I crossed it in first and I was Paralympic champion.

For four years I had imagined what winning this race would feel like several times a day. Every time I walked the dog, I had pictured this moment and how it would feel.

But now it was here. I had done it and it was nothing like I'd imagined at all.

I just felt relief. There had been so much pressure on me. I was just grateful that I had performed.

I made a point of seeing the other athletes and shaking their hands. But then came the part I had been waiting for and I ran the 20 metres or so to where my friends and family were in the stands and saw Victoria crying. Looking around, I suddenly realised quite how many of my friends had come along, and quite how many of those big, burly Essex boys were crying their eyes out too. It just felt surreal.

It was with family and friends that I was happiest – I felt safe. I'd only been there a few moments when one of my mates threw a Union Jack down to me. Straight away I was off again, draping the flag over my shoulders to pose for photos before setting off with it on my lap of honour.

As soon as I left my friends I was totally out of my comfort zone. I didn't really know what to do while jogging round the track. I'd spent years looking forward to this moment and all I really wanted to do was enjoy it with my mates. Instead I was out on the track again, feeling quite lonely.

I had prepared for every aspect of the race, but had done nothing to prepare for this bit. I wouldn't say I didn't enjoy the lap of honour, but I certainly wasn't comfortable with it. I remember self-consciously waving at the crowd, just hoping they would wave back.

If my mates could have come round with me I would have loved every minute, but as it was I spent the whole lap just waiting to get back to my family where I could feel safe again and start celebrating properly. But before I even completed a full lap to make it back to them, I was taken away to prepare for my medal ceremony.

I was led to a back room, where we went through several formalities. I got my accreditations back and we ran through what would happen in the presentation itself. I then just had to wait for the ceremony to begin.

My ceremony came round comparatively quickly. I felt more ready for this than the lap of honour and was determined to enjoy myself. The pressure of the race was over and all I had to do was collect my medal.

I stood, excited, on the edge of the track as the music started to play. They announced the medal ceremony for the Men's T46 800 metres and the dignitaries led me out to the rostrum, accompanied by some ladies carrying the medals on cushions and others with flowers.

We were called in reverse order, so I waited behind the podium while the Rwandan Jean de Dieu Nkundabera and Nouioua stepped up to receive bronze and silver respectively.

And then the moment I had waited so long for. The announcement went round the stadium, "Gold medalist, representing Great Britain and Northern Ireland, Danny Crates."

I stepped up, bent forward and felt the medal as they placed it round my neck. I was given a bunch of flowers and, for the Athens Games, laurel wreaths were put on our heads too.

I was looking for my family in the crowd, but they had stayed where they had watched the race, in the far end of the stadium. While I was looking, the national anthem started.

I suddenly realised that all the cameras would be on me and, again, I wasn't comfortable. I've never really been a performer and hadn't enjoyed being the centre of attention since my school days. I was happy to attract attention through my sporting achievements, but not in day-to-day life.

I didn't know what to do as the anthem played, whether I should be singing, looking thoughtful or just pleased. Again, I just wanted to get back to my family so I could relax and allow myself to enjoy what I had achieved.

Once the anthem was over we had more photos taken on the podium before, finally, I could get back to see everyone. That was the most amazing feeling, trying to walk back through the crowds at the back of the stadium. I had a medal on so everyone wanted to speak to me or to get an autograph, but I just wanted to get round to where I knew my family were waiting.

I walked down the steps from the top of the stadium, with my medal round my neck and a bunch of flowers in my hand. My mates didn't see me at first, but as I got nearer, one of them turned round. Within seconds everyone was going mad. That was the start of one hell of a party.

Everyone was there: Victoria, Mum and Dad, Paul and Katie, Ayo, all these friends who for so long had just accepted that I was a professional athlete and that I couldn't go on big nights out and boys' holidays with them.

I had missed their birthdays and weddings because they hadn't fitted in with my training schedule, but they never questioned it and never tried to talk me out of going training so I could go out drinking and, best of all, they were all there with me to see it all pay off.

My mates never put pressure on me to be anything other than an athlete and, as soon as I had my chance to be one, they were there to support me. I guess the fact they got to go on a two-day drinking holiday while they were supporting me probably made coming along an easier decision for most of them. Some of them started drinking at my heat at 9 o'clock on the Friday morning and then just kept going until long after the final on the Saturday night.

I did a few interviews before leaving the stadium and then got the bus back to my family's hotel with everyone else. I was still wearing my Great Britain tracksuit and medal, so people kept coming up for photos and autographs.

I nearly ended up wearing the tracksuit all night. I had always planned to go out with my friends and family after the race, win or lose, and Victoria had brought a bag of my clothes to the stadium so I wouldn't have to go back to the village to change. But in the excitement after my race, she left the bag in the stadium, so once we got to the hotel I had to beg, steal or borrow whatever – probably dirty – clothes my mates would spare.

Once I'd got changed we all went up to the roof bar and just had a fantastic evening. A load of the crew and commentators from the BBC who I knew at the time came back as well, including Stuart Storey and Paul Dickenson, who had given me such a hard time in Sydney.

I found it hard to celebrate though. Everyone around me was going mad and we all really enjoyed the night, but I hadn't really comprehended what had happened yet. Winning that race was so important to me and I'd worked so hard to get it, but I hadn't yet had time to sit down, take a deep breath and get my head round the fact I had actually done it.

The next morning I woke up with a slightly sorer head than I'd gone to bed with. Victoria and I walked up to the Acropolis with a few friends. Up there, we just messed around. I had the medal with me and my mates were all having photographs taken with it. The medal attracted all sorts of attention and tourists started coming over to talk to us. My mates all trying to blag it, telling the tourists that they had won the medal and persuading them to pose for photos with them. It was hilarious to watch and that's when I really started to enjoy myself.

I had to go to the studios to do an interview with Clare Balding on the BBC. I actually enjoyed that bit of limelight. I had done a pre-race interview with Colin Jackson at the Panathinaikos stadium in Athens, but the post-race interview is a lot easier to enjoy when everything has gone well.

We talked about the race and watched it back. I remember thinking, "I've made it now." I believed my life was going to change because I was now a Paralympic champion.

Of course, the same thing happens whether you win or not. Nothing changes. My room was still a mess, nobody was going to clean it up for me. Whether I had a gold medal or not, my mates would still pick me up when I was down and put me down when I was up.

Even so, I'd had a great time in Athens. I had won on the biggest stage there is and was the only British endurance athlete to win a medal at all at the Games. When the closing ceremony came round I made sure I made the most of the celebrations.

I flew back to the UK with the rest of the team the next day. Then it was back to everyday life again.

First though, there was some celebrating to be done. I still had the champagne that the Winston Churchill Trust had presented to me after my scuba diving course seven years earlier. My parents had suggested we drink it when I got back from Sydney, but I had told them bronze wasn't enough.

Now though, I thought I had done something to justify opening it, so we invited a few people who had been really special in my life over. John Keefe was there, along with Kevin Lidlow and his wife, Kim, and obviously I wanted my family there too. It was all the people who had stood by me. We opened the champagne and had a toast, not just to what I had achieved, but to the help each of them had given me in achieving it.

My mates also organised a massive party to celebrate. They put on loads of food and music and invited all my friends and family to the

Havencrest, the local bar where I used to drink. It was the perfect way to round off the whole 2004 Paralympics and allowed me to share the experience with everybody.

That they went to the trouble of organising that night after so many had also travelled out to Athens too just made it all the more special. It also gave me a chance to make up for a few of the nights out I had missed. I did my best that night to catch up on all of the drinking that my training schedule had forced me to miss during the previous four years.

The final celebration was on a slightly bigger scale as I took part in the post-Olympic victory parade through London. Thousands of people lined the streets as we took a series of floats up Oxford Street, down through Piccadilly Circus and round Trafalgar Square.

As an athlete you worry if anybody is going to turn out to see you, but the response we got was overwhelming.

The day ended with the obligatory visit to Buckingham Palace where, as a gold medalist, I was introduced to the Queen. This time I made a point of remembering my encounter with a royal.

Chapter 11
How do you top the best year of your life?

Even if my life hadn't changed I expected my professional career to pick up off the back of Athens. I had been working as a speaker for four years now and that was still going well. But I had enjoyed a much higher profile as a potential gold medalist in the run-up to the Games and I assumed I would be inundated with all sorts of glamorous offers now I was an actual champion. That never really materialised.

My raised profile did give me some status as a minor celebrity though, and I enjoyed a few of the perks that went with that. I was invited to *BBC Sports Personality of the Year* and started getting booked for a handful of TV shows. I did *A Question of Sport* twice and also found myself appearing on daytime TV shows like Channel 5's *The Wright Stuff.*

I even did *Celebrity Ready Steady Cook* where I was a green pepper against one of the wheelchair basketball team's red tomato. I was paired with Kevin Woodford and we made a chicken dish that he christened 'Olympicnic'. Most importantly, we won.

A personal highlight was being asked to open a local Indian restaurant, the Bikash Tandoori House in Corringham. One of my tracksuits is still up on their wall.

Closer to athletics, I was able to use my profile as an official ambassador for the London 2012 Olympic Bid. The bid team had realised that getting the British public excited about anything was a tall order, never mind something that might not happen and wouldn't arrive for another seven years even if it did.

I went out visiting schools and events throughout the UK. As someone who had been there, I explained what hosting the Games brings to a city and just tried to whip up some enthusiasm for the bid. I really enjoyed playing a part in the whole process and was particularly excited to get the chance to meet Lord Sebastian Coe, who was overseeing the whole operation. When I was running 800 and 1500 metres as a 10-year-old, he was the best in the world over both distances. I relished the chance to work with him on the 2012 bid.

My personal part in the campaign culminated in Trafalgar Square on 6 July 2005, the day of the announcement. I was on a stage with Steve Cram and Dame Kelly Holmes in front of a big screen that was broadcasting the announcement live from Singapore, where Seb and the rest of the bid team had flown out for the final presentations and some last minute campaigning.

It was fairly quiet early on and we felt a bit silly standing around waiting. I don't think anyone really believed we were going to win it at that stage. That doubt had probably been behind a lot of the public's apathy during the campaign.

As the day went on, the rival cities were eliminated one by one. But after each round of votes, London was still in it and I think belief started to grow. Certainly the numbers in Trafalgar Square steadily grew as first Moscow and then New York were knocked out. When Madrid went too I think it started to occur to people that there might be a party after all.

Without Madrid, it was down to just Paris and London. Paris had led throughout, but we expected to pick up a lot of Madrid's votes. Suddenly Trafalgar Square was heaving.

Paris was probably still the favourite and as Jacques Rogge, the president of the International Olympic Committee, started to make the announcement I was already consoling myself and thinking we'd done well to get down to the final two.

I think Kelly and Steve might have been thinking the same because when the announcement came – "the games of the 30th Olympiad are awarded to… London" – we all went absolutely berserk on the stage, completely forgetting the thousands of people in the crowd. The picture of the three of us leaping in the air has become one of the iconic images of the day and sums up the absolute euphoria of that moment.

The bombings the next day brought the city crashing down from its high. It took a long time for London to get over that and for the 2012 momentum to pick up again.

I was increasingly busy off the track, but had to remember that I was primarily an athlete and couldn't let myself get too distracted. I had resumed training a month after coming back from Athens and was keen to get out and race again.

The first major tournament was the inaugural Paralympic Word Cup, the first of what would become an annual event in the City of Manchester Stadium.

I was on a home track and had won Paralympic gold in my last major race. The result should have been a formality, but I was caught off guard. Samir Nouioua got some revenge, taking me 150 metres from the line and leaving me with just a silver medal.

The result was a big blow and served as a bit of an eye-opener. I don't know if I'd become complacent, but if I had, that was the kick I needed. It had taken me seven years to get to the top but I realised then that I wouldn't have as long to work out how to stay there.

The European Championships in Helsinki later that year presented my first opportunity to get my career back on track, although the Algerian Nouioua would not be there.

Even without him and the other non-European athletes, it turned out I would have to go through quite a lot to defend my European title. As we were waiting in the call room before the final, an almighty thunderstorm was brewing.

As the race before ours finished, the heavens opened and a gale force wind blew across the stadium. The 800 metres final was postponed as a result, but as we had already gone into the call room, we would not be allowed to leave. That storm added 40 minutes to the time we would have to wait before racing.

I was already nervous and any extra time in that enclosed space, with just my rivals for company, was going to seriously test my ability to maintain focus. I laid on the floor and wrapped myself up in coats just to try to take myself away from everything. Somehow I managed to nod off.

Eventually the weather cleared and they came to take us out onto a wet track. Seven athletes were led out but I was still on the floor, under the coats.

Generally I always preferred to walk out on to the track first. That was where I wanted to be at the end of the race so I might as well get there early. But this time I wasn't walking out at all.

My parents noticed from the stands that I was missing. Apparently my mum assumed I had the hump and was refusing to come out.

Thankfully I woke up and realised what had happened, running down to the stadium and making it onto the track in time for the race to begin. As we stood in our lanes, waiting to be called to the start line, a massive bolt of lightning hit the field next to the stadium. A gust of wind shot through the stadium and a marquee in the middle of the track blew over, landing just feet away from us near the finish line.

We were all called off the track for safety reasons, taken to another holding area and the race was postponed again.

While we were in the holding area, I needed to go to the toilet and had to ask an official to escort me. While I was in there the weather cleared, and seven athletes went back to the start line without me again.

My superstition about being the first out onto the track had been well and truly scuppered. I wasn't just the last on to the track, I didn't emerge until several minutes after all the other competitors, twice.

I did make it to the start line though and, despite the worst build-up to a race of my entire career I won fairly easily. I was still smarting from the defeat to Nouioua in Manchester though, and a European gold was hardly a consolation.

I was determined there would be no more slips in 2006, but there was another complication to overcome first. From a young age I had noticed that my calves would often twitch, moving all on their own and generally looking like something from a science fiction film. After Athens, I noticed this was getting worse. The doctors call the condition vesiculation, it was just nerves letting off a bit of steam, but mine was quite severe.

To start with, I'd thought it was quite funny, pointing it out to my mates whenever it happened, but now it was causing me to cramp, which meant I often couldn't run and had to cut my training short. It seemed to be worst when I was doing quicker sessions.

I had many tests and tried different medications in an attempt to at least control it. I even had a biopsy where they took a bit of my calf muscle to be analysed. But they couldn't find any way to help. It just became something else I would have to deal with and learn to train around.

I found it helped to keep moving, so when I finished a repetition, I couldn't let myself sit around and let my muscles relax at all. The problem only ever affected me in training and never in races, but it stayed with me throughout the rest of my athletics career.

Before the 2006 season began, I heard that Paul Pearce had died. I was training on my own the day before my birthday, running through the woods when I got the phone call telling me he had been hit by a van while out running on the roads.

Since dragging us all along with his infectious enthusiasm in Athens Paul had consistently been the life and soul of the Paralympic team. Becoming a Paralympian had meant so much to him and really changed his life. He was a genuinely special person and is still missed by everyone.

When I got back to competitive running, the season started with an 800 metres gold at the second Paralympic World Cup in Manchester. That went some way to putting my defeat the previous year behind me, but there was a bigger event on the horizon in the form of the World Championships in Assen.

I felt I had a point to prove at World Championships in general. This would be my third appearance at the event and I had no individual medals to show from my previous two having finished last in the 400-metre final in 1998 and fourth in both the 400 and 800 metres in 2002.

My success in Manchester at the start of the season meant that, with my Paralympic and European titles, I had now won gold at every other major event. The World Championships was the only one missing from my collection but I knew in the back of my mind that this would probably be my last chance to win there.

In Athens and Sydney, my nerves had built to the point where I felt physically sick for a week before the race. For the 2006 World Championships I had the same sensation for four weeks beforehand. I had a room to myself in Assen and shut myself away the whole time I was there.

I hardly sleep a wink the night before the final. I dreamt that I fell asleep at the Dartford Tunnel tollbooth, so I must have nodded off at least briefly, but I woke up exhausted and was still tired as I stood on the start line hours later.

The race went well, I was in my usual position at the front of the pack early on. As we came to the end of the first lap the Ukrainian, Oleh

Leshchyshyn, and the Pole, Marcin Awiżeń, came through on the inside to take the lead.

As we went through the bell I did my usual "wake up" routine, but I kicked a little too hard. I went right round the outside of them both and shot off into the lead by about four metres.

I'd been too bold, but once you do something like that in a big international race, you can't backtrack and let them reel you back in. I couldn't show any weakness so I had to stretch it out and keep going for all of the remaining 400 metres.

I spent the whole last lap hoping I hadn't gone too early. Thankfully I hadn't. I crossed the line first in 1 minute, 54.92 seconds to complete my set of gold medals, beating the Kenyan Stephen Wambua and Awiżeń into second and third respectively.

Nouioua finished out of the medals but, after the race, the Algerian showed me a bit of respect for the first time in my career. He came over to shake my hand and we had some photos taken together. He had always blanked me before, whether I had beaten him or not. I can only assume his new-found respect was down to the fact I had completed the full set of gold medals.

All of my old rivals seemed to be seeing me in a new light. After the race I was in for drug testing with Oumar Basakoulba Kone, the Ivorian whose world record I had taken and the athlete I most feared and respected during my career.

My doctor spoke French so for the first time I was able to have a basic conversation with Kone. Having done the set I was pleased to be able to tell him he had been my main target on the track. We bonded and he even gave me a vest, which he told me to give to Victoria because it wouldn't fit me.

When I first got into the sport I had thought him arrogant, but that was probably just because I didn't understand him. I soon worked out he wasn't arrogant at all, just crazy.

Away from the track, I was awarded an honorary doctorate from Essex University for services to sport. My family like to point out that most people have to study for at least four years to get that sort of qualification, while I just had to run round a track a few times before I got given one.

Whether or not the award was merited, I am officially Doctor Danny Crates, although I've never actually used the title.

The year ended on a personal high. Once the athletics season was out of the way I was planning a wedding. I had always told Victoria that I was too busy preparing for the Paralympics to consider getting married, but I promised her we would get engaged after the Games.

When I came back from Athens, she was quick to remind me of this. I tried to say I hadn't specified which Paralympics, but she wasn't having it.

Long before I got round to popping the question, Victoria had told me what ring I should buy, the size I should buy it in and the shop where I could go to to get it, just in case I ever wanted to buy an engagement ring. She had apparently spent the previous year trying it on in the jewellers near where she worked.

When it came to proposing, I rang Victoria's dad to ask his permission. He didn't take long to say, "Yes, you can have her."

It seemed he couldn't wait for me to take her off his hands. He rang me back 10 minutes later to check if I'd asked her yet.

I like to think that the proposal itself was romantic, but I'm not sure if came across that way. Our dog, Kitty, a white lurcher, was always seen as Victoria's baby, so I wanted to include her somehow.

Having bought the ring, I placed it between Kitty's front paws. I then casually said, "Oh, I think the dog's got something for you."

Victoria saw the ring and said "yes". We were straight on the phone to our parents and they all came over to help celebrate. Everyone started getting excitable, talking about going to wedding fairs and choosing a venue, flowers, food and all the other stuff you need to arrange. That was my moment to remind them all that in a few days, I would be going to America for four weeks' of warm weather training.

I don't know whether proposing just before that trip to America was coincidence or just good planning – I guess the answer depends on if you're male or female.

On 9 December 2006 we got married in a beautiful location, a big country estate in Essex. All my friends and family were there. Unfortunately a few of my rugby mates were there too. In the morning, we were all running round trying to get the last few things organised. All the family was helping out, but my dad kept disappearing. Whenever we found him he had a smile on his face.

As the day went on, he kept disappearing, each time coming back with a broader grin and rosier cheeks. Eventually we found out he had been popping up to the rugby boys' rooms where they were all enjoying a little pre-wedding aperitif.

The day after the wedding, Victoria and I jetted off to Kenya for a safari before going onto Zanzibar, just off Tanzania, where we spent Christmas. It was perfect.

As soon as we were married, we started talking about having kids. Victoria wanted to start straight away, but I was reluctant: "If we conceive now," I told her, "it will arrive right in the middle of the athletics season. We need to plan this."

I was free to concentrate on my running, but at the end of a season that saw me retain my Paralympic World Cup title, the real highlight came in October 2007 when my first son Henry was born. He was six weeks premature, but he still managed to arrive late enough not to disrupt my training.

For someone who needed to be so controlled and structured in every aspect of my professional life, I was hopelessly unprepared for childbirth.

As Victoria went into labour I had no bag packed and was nowhere near finishing the nursery. I was in a daze as we drove to hospital and had no idea what was going on. I actually stopped on the way to hospital so I could fill up with petrol. I then left Victoria waiting in the car so I could pop to a cashpoint. Not for the first time, I must have driven her mad.

Because Henry arrived so early, when we got to the hospital they did everything they could to stop the labour. Victoria was up and down, on and off the labour ward for four days before he was finally born.

He was taken to the special care baby unit, which was tough for all three of us, but everything turned out OK.

At the time I was sponsored by Vauxhall, but I'd got about as far with my plans to switch to a family car as I had with painting the nursery and was driving a convertible Astra. I remember going to pick Henry and Victoria up from the hospital with my brother, Paul. The two of us were in the car park trying to fit the child seat into the car but the only way we could do it was by putting the roof down.

Paul and I were both stood in the back of this boy racer's car, trying to work out which straps went where so the seat would stay where we put it. If any of the midwives had looked out of the window and seen the mess we were in, I don't think they would have let us take Henry home at all.

Chapter 12
Testing times

It is often said that it's hard to win a title, but even harder to defend one. In 2008 I would go to the Beijing Paralympics as reigning champion and I was determined to do everything I could to add a second Paralympic gold to my collection.

The year began with a spell away from my new family as I flew out to Potchefstroom in South Africa for some warm weather training in preparation for Beijing. I spent two weeks there in January and it was the best camp I had ever been to. I felt like I was in the shape of my life. Things couldn't have been better.

Pretty much the entire Great Britain athletics team was out there and I was training with the usual crowd from Ayo's stable including Donna Fraser and Marilyn Okoro.

It's just a lovely way to train with no distractions. I would spend breakfast discussing the day's schedule with my mates, then get out to actually do my training routine before breaking in the afternoon to have tea in the café overlooking the grass track where I would just sit and watch Mo Farah and the other long-distance runners going through their drills.

We'd head back to the hotel, eat dinner and then, as middle-distance runners, we'd go out to run again in the evening. I loved it. This was what being a full-time athlete was all about. The sort of experience I enjoyed in Potchefstroom made all those winter runs in the snow and rain in England worthwhile.

Everything was falling into place. I knew I had never put in better training sessions in my life. I was getting faster and faster, stronger and stronger.

In the evenings, Ayo gave us regular training reviews in the hotel. I'd sat in front of him so many times and he always started in the same way, "Now, Dan," before going on to tell me off about something.

But when we sat down at the end of the two weeks in South Africa he told me, "You're just too quick. You are running too fast. I have got to slow you down."

That meant my training was going to get a bit more arduous. He was going to lengthen my routines. I was on such a high and running so well that my body was naturally trying to go even faster, but it just wasn't right for me to be going as quick as I was in January.

I left the camp feeling really positive. I was in the best shape I had ever been in and came back to the UK with the sole intention of knuckling down and preparing for Beijing.

In March I went in to the lab for a physiological test. I had to undergo these twice a year and had hated it at first. I was naturally sceptical and didn't really get it. In the lab someone would stick pins in my ears until they drew blood before making me run on a treadmill until I reached exhaustion. They would watch my reaction to all this, then invariably set my training goals higher.

I had no understanding of what they were doing or why and never really engaged with the process. It became a game of cat and mouse with the physiologists whenever they tried to get me in to the lab. They even agreed that I wouldn't have to undergo the tests as often as the other athletes.

I felt I knew my body well enough. It was something we had always worked on in training. If I went to Ayo at the start of a session and told him I didn't feel too great he would just ask me what I was doing there at all; If I got hurt and said I'd felt a twinge a couple of reps earlier, he would have no sympathy.

Ayo had always encouraged us to respond to whatever our bodies were telling us and trusted us to know what we were capable of doing.

That approach had probably led to my initial scepticism about physiology. I was happy doing it the old-fashioned way with Ayo, letting him set my weights programme, my training routine and everything else.

Ayo would have been happy for me to embrace all the technology available; several of his other athletes took full advantage of physiology as well as psychology, sports psychiatry, speed training and conditioning. But I thought running was just running, putting one foot in front of the other, and I found the other stuff tough.

One day I was in a training session with Jo Fenn and I saw she had a really swanky polar heart-rate monitor on. I asked where she'd got it and she told me the physiologist had given it to her. That swung it for me. Suddenly I could see the appeal of going to the lab.

I phoned Charlie Pedlar, the physiologist, and said, "Charlie, where's my watch?"

He told me, "But you won't use it, you're not into this stuff."

I just said, "I am now."

So on the promise that I would use it, I got my own heart-rate monitor. Slowly I started to get the whole thing and actually embraced what Charlie and his team were trying to do.

By the time we got to 2008, I had been engaged with the programme long enough to have results going back several years. That meant the tests I had that March could confirm what I already felt.

Charlie told me, "Dan, you have never been fitter, never been faster, and never been stronger in your entire career."

I went in to training the next day feeling unbeatable. We were doing 400-metre repetitions on the track. I was due to do 13 laps with a one minute rest in between each 400-metre run. This was a massive session but I did it and, again, did it better than I had ever done before.

Every repetition was my quickest ever. Most significantly my times were consistent throughout without dying off at all. The last 400 metres was quicker than the first.

I'd felt a slight soreness in my back in the days leading up to that session so when I finished running I went to see the physio, Mark Young, to get it checked out. As an arm amputee I was prone to back trouble and I'd had a few small issues throughout my career so I wasn't worried.

I lay on the bed and explained that it felt a bit 'twingey', pointing out where it was hurting. Mark pressed the spot and, bang – I went into a spasm on the bed with shooting pains through my back and legs. I was left in agony, unable to move.

The doctors gave me some strong painkillers and I laid there for two hours before the pain subsided. There was nothing more they could do then. We would all have to wait a couple of days for the inflammation to die down so I could have a scan.

I had to stop training and, 48 hours later, went in for what would turn out to be the first of far too many scans that year. The MRI revealed a small tear in a disc in my spine.

A torn disc probably sounds worse than it is. It certainly felt worse. It wasn't a big tear though, so the doctors and physios suggested I just rest for 10 days and then gradually ease myself back into my training.

It didn't feel like anything more than a minor setback. Sometimes an injury like that can actually benefit you because it stops you from training for a while. Often you've got injured because you've overtrained and the injury is your body's way of forcing you to slow down.

If it's a minor injury and you don't have to break from training for long you usually come back feeling better than you did before. The biggest problem I had was that the injury would mean an enforced spell of rehab. I would have to spend most of my days in the gym doing strength-building exercises when I just wanted to run.

I hated being injured but the back injury made me think I might have been pushing myself a little too hard. I took it as a warning, but it had come at the right time – I still had a long way to go before Beijing.

Within two weeks of the injury I was back to full training and running full speed. I was injury-free and everything was back on course for the Paralympics.

During April the Olympic torch relay came through London on its way to Beijing and I was selected to be one of the torch bearers. I saw it as a great honour because, for me, the flame really represents the Games. Seeing the flame really drove home the fact that a Paralympics was on the way.

I was given a fairly prominent leg, running just outside the Millennium Dome where the UK leg of the relay would end with a huge celebratory concert.

It would not be straightforward though. There was a lot of controversy about Beijing hosting the Olympics and Paralympics at all due to the Chinese government's human rights record. The whole relay was targeted by protestors and my leg – in an open space on live TV – provided them with a perfect platform.

I arrived by the Dome early to be briefed on our strictly timetabled movements. Dame Ellen MacArthur would bring the torch up the river by boat before running up the jetty to hand it to me. I would then carry it towards the Dome and hand it over to Theo Walcott for the penultimate leg. He would give it to Dame Kelly Holmes who would take it into the venue and light the cauldron to start the concert.

When we saw our positions, we realised we couldn't wear our kit until the last minute because there were too many protestors about. Finally, when we couldn't leave it any longer, we put our tracksuits on.

I then just had to wait. There were a lot of well-wishers who had come to see the flame on its journey through London, but they weren't making anywhere near as much noise as the protestors.

It was weird. I could understand and sympathise with what they were protesting about, but I believe the Olympic and Paralympic games should just be about sport with no political agendas; people and countries coming together to try to be the best they can be.

I remember Mum and Dad were standing in the crowd, but everyone else seemed to be there to protest and they obviously knew who the various runners were for the different stages. They started shouting things like, "Danny Crates, you should be ashamed of yourself."

I was just thinking, "There are a lot of things I have done in my life that I should be ashamed of, but this is not one of them."

Then I saw the boat coming up the Thames. It was only when Ellen MacArthur stepped onto the jetty that I realised the level of security. She was surrounded by a ring of security men, who had accompanied the flame all the way from China. Around them was a ring of police. You couldn't see her at all. All I could see was a flame sticking out of the top of this moving crowd.

As it approached, the flame attendant who had been waiting with me switched on the gas in my torch so it would take the flame. As Ellen got very near, the front of this ring of security opened up so she could meet me before closing up around both of us.

I lit my torch and, as I started to run away, the police and security men at the back opened up to leave Dame Ellen behind before closing around me again. I didn't think too much about the arrangement at this point. I was too busy making sure I savoured every moment of the experience. I knew the next time I saw that flame would be Beijing 2008.

I reached Theo Walcott and the same thing happened with the security ring opening up and closing around us. But as Theo ran off the security went with him and I was on my own, surrounded by lots of angry protestors, wearing a bright white tracksuit and holding an unlit torch just in case there was any doubt who I was and what I was doing there.

I turned round and saw Ellen MacArthur had kept running after I'd left her in the same position and had just about caught me up. Soon we were both running together shouting, "Wait for us!" as we chased Theo Walcott.

Of course, within minutes, Theo had joined us and the three of us were all trying to catch up with Kelly Holmes to stay out of harm's way. We had no chance.
Fortunately we found a friendly policeman who escorted us into the Dome and away from the crowd outside.

Despite the distractions, the torch relay made me redouble my efforts. I threw myself back into training to make sure I would see the flame again.

In May I was doing 200-metre reps, a similar routine to the one I had been doing immediately prior to the back problem flaring up. During the session I felt a bit of pain in my calf, but I told myself it was nothing and shrugged it off.

A few days later I flew out to Ireland with the rest of the family to celebrate my dad's 60th birthday. I got off the plane, arrived at the bungalow where we were all staying and went out for a run. But while I was out I felt more pains in my calf. They were so bad I had to stop and walk back.

I still didn't really think a lot of it but spoke to the physios as soon as I was back in the UK. They had a look and my second MRI scan of the season revealed I had torn my soleus, a muscle just below my calf. Again this wasn't a massive injury but it was now May and the Paralympics were only four months away. Another spell of physio and rehab followed but, again, I was back on the track within a couple of weeks.

This time though, far from coming back refreshed and ready, I was finding running difficult. Every time I tried to run I struggled and, as time went on, I was getting more stressed by my lack of progress.

I was still in rehab, and I was still hating it. My training consisted of spending all morning on an exercise bike, trying to mirror the routine that my training group was doing on the track. If they were doing sprints I would put in equivalent times sprinting on the bike. I'd then do weights in the afternoon, go home to rest and then come back to the gym in the evening to get back on the bike for a 30-minute steady 'run'.

I got so bored of being in the gym and UK Athletics must have got fed up with me moaning about it because they quickly decided I should be allowed to use a proper bike and do my exercises out in the fresh air.

My training and rehab programme then took a strange turn. I was out in the garden one day, telling my next-door neighbour, Chris Spooner, about the cycling. He just said, "I'll come out with you."

I had been training for eight or nine years with the absolute elite of the athletics world, but I now found my Paralympic hopes resting on me cycling round Essex with the bloke next door.

To be fair, he used to ride to work every day and was pretty good on a bike so whenever he could, he'd come out training with me. He'd come home from work and we'd go straight out on a bike ride together.

Chris was really into his cycling and had this top-end mountain bike with all the gear, but I just had this cheap bike and I couldn't get near him. Eventually UK Athletics bought me this lightweight mountain bike that had been adapted for me to ride and I got a bit closer to him. Then we fitted it with road tyres and I was even quicker. Clip pedals then allowed me to drive a lot harder. After a while, Chris couldn't get near me.

We both really used to push it and I really enjoyed it. It was a great way to train, so much better than being stuck in a gym, but deep down I just wanted to run.

I was still having regular scans. There were numerous medical interventions and cortisone injections into my achilles. I saw just about every specialist in the country but didn't seem to be getting any better. We got to late June and I still wasn't running.

Now missing Beijing was looking more likely than going and I was starting to get panicky. I never admitted it to anyone else, but I was terrified I wasn't going to get there.

I was still the champion and desperately wanted to defend my title. The shape I had been in three months earlier made it all the more frustrating. I also had a number of sponsorship contracts that would make winning in Beijing very worthwhile financially, but suddenly nothing seemed to be working

In June I suffered another setback as I redamaged my soleus and my achilles. I knew I wouldn't be able to run again until late July and making the Paralympics was looking even more unlikely.

In desperation I took the decision to change tack and try something completely different. The medical team around me had been fantastic but they had tried everything they could think of and we didn't seem to be getting anywhere.

They did have one last trick up their sleeve though, and sent me to see a specialist in London who delivered a high volume injection into my achilles. It was quite a radical treatment that had only been used on a handful of footballers before and not really on any athletes. Under ultrasound they injected a mixture of saline, anti-inflammatories and cortisone into my achilles.

It was a high volume injection so it made my whole calf swell up. The aim was to strip all the tendons off the sheath, to free everything up and let it heal cleanly. I then had to wait 10 days before I could even try to run.

I found a new physio, Paul Martin, who worked with the Paralympic swimming team. He was based in St Mary's out near Twickenham so I would go and stay at the Lensbury Club where the England rugby team often stayed and I'd train from there for a few days at a time while seeing him.

The physiologist was also based out that way and I would see him while I was out there. He had a fantastic device called a G-trainer, which had originally been devised by NASA to enable astronauts to train for space, but had been tweaked so we could use it to run at a reduced body weight.

There were only three in the world at the time and it basically consisted of a treadmill with this big skirt around it with some fitted shorts in the centre. When I stepped into the shorts and zipped myself in it created a sealed unit. The physiologists could then inflate the skirt to adjust the weight I was running at.

I started running at 20% of my own bodyweight. It was a strange sensation. I could feel the force of the air pushing in on my legs, but it was lifting me at the same time, taking 80% of my weight so I felt really light. However weird it felt, it meant I was running again.

Soon I was running at 80% of my bodyweight on the G-trainer and I was still doing my bike training and seeing Paul, who had a completely new approach to treating my injuries.

Everything I was doing was going well and it felt like I was finally moving in the right direction, although I still hadn't run outside of the G-trainer and was not yet anywhere near confident I was going to make Beijing. We were in July and I hadn't even been near a track to get the necessary qualifying times. Still, I allowed a bit of optimism to creep in.

Towards the end of July, the Great Britain Paralympics team had its final squad get together in Birmingham. This weekend is the only time outside of the Games that the whole team would be in one place. The event is an opportunity to sort out final briefings, the team photo and other formalities, before finishing with a big gala dinner.

During the weekend we would be given our kit for the forthcoming Games. In 1998 I had been given one t-shirt, one pair of shorts and one tracksuit. Now we had wetsuits, tracksuits, socks, walking-out suits and about 20 t-shirts each.

The whole team gathered in this huge room to receive their kit. We could change any item of kit that needed changing and an army of tailors was on hand in case anything needed adjustments. That's the point where a lot of the athletes start to get excited.

While I was there the nominations for flag bearer in the opening ceremony were announced. The honour would be decided by the entire team voting for one name from a list of about 12 nominees. My name was on the list.

Normally they would announce who had won the vote at the gala dinner, but in 2008 they decided to wait until just before the Games. They didn't say why, but I couldn't help clinging on to the hope that they were waiting to see if I would be fit enough to get to Beijing. If I needed any more motivation to try to get myself there, that was it.

At the end of the weekend, just before we were about to leave, I was down in the kit room with a few others who had altered clothes to collect. Someone, who was not a permanent member of the Paralympic Association but was just helping out with kit, came over and whispered in my ear that they were taking my kit back because they didn't think I was going to make it to the Games.

That, there and then, destroyed me.

Another athlete overheard the conversation and went to tell a more senior member of the team what had been said. Straight away they came over to apologise and tell me that should never have happened.

What really hurt was that, even if the way I'd been told was unprofessional and hurtful, I knew what I'd been told was right. I've always believed that you shouldn't have that kit unless you've earned it, and at that point, I hadn't. To me the kit I had been given was worthless unless I could go to Beijing and race in it.

The weekend came to an end and everybody said their goodbyes, but I didn't go home. Instead I left the kit behind and drove straight to the Alexandra Stadium in Birmingham, the venue where I had raced in my first international competition a decade earlier.

I put on my trainers thinking, "It's kill or cure now."

They had told me I wasn't going to Beijing unless I could run, so I was going to run.

I jogged a warm-up lap of the field outside the stadium and then just kept going, getting quicker and quicker with each lap. I ran for half an hour until I realised I could run through the pain. It was the first time in two months I had run without the help of the G-trainer.

Suddenly my dream was alive again. Although any excitement was tempered by a concern that I had lost four or five months of serious training and I still felt the weight of expectation. Getting to Beijing alone was not enough, I was expected to go there and win.

I went straight back into training and just kept building it up until, just 10 days after that run in Birmingham, I was on the start line for a competitive race, a BMC 800 metres in Eton. It wasn't fast and it wasn't pretty. I ran it one hundredth of a second under two minutes, the second slowest time of my career and way off the standard I needed for the Paralympics, but at last I was running.

I received a further boost with the news that I had been selected for the Paralympic team on the back of my times from the previous season. The announcement was made and my kit was, belatedly, sent out to me.

My second race back – another BMC event in Eltham, South London – came 11 days after the first. There I ran 1 minute, 57.47 seconds. I was progressing, but it still wasn't quick enough.

At this stage, I had about four weeks before I would have to race at the Paralympics, but just a few days before I would have to fly out to the pre-camp.

Whilst doing a warm down after that race in Eltham I felt some twinges in my right achilles and calf. Again I pushed any doubts to one side and got on the plane that would take me to the pre-Games camp in Macau.

I spent the flight trying to remain positive and to forget the amount of training I had missed. But however focused I was, it was difficult not to worry about my lack of preparation.

The holding camp was another five-star resort equipped with everything we could possibly need. I had been to a training camp at the same venue in 2007, albeit reluctantly. When asked if I wanted to come out with some other athletes to familiarise ourselves with the facility, I was initially unsure whether to go. I felt I was already used to warm weather training and, as Victoria was pregnant at the time, getting a preview of the resort didn't seem essential.

The team managers had previously respected mine and Ayo's judgement, but this time they insisted I went. As soon as I got there I was happy to have been forced. It really opened my eyes to the conditions we would face in Beijing and enabled me to have a clearer idea of the heat and humidity we would have to race in.

As soon as I arrived in Macau for the holding camp, I dumped my bags in my room and went straight out for a jog to recover from the flight and to start the acclimatisation process. I had planned a three-mile route round a clifftop at the top of a reservoir, high up in the mountains. Half a mile in I felt another stabbing pain in my right achilles and found myself hobbling back to the hotel.

I went straight to the physios and had yet another MRI scan – I lost count of how many I had that year – but they couldn't work out what was wrong.

Two days later I was training on the track. The team had come up with a controlled programme, a series of drills that they hoped would encourage everything to settle down enough for me to resume my original schedule.

After a while they wanted me to try running, but every time I did, the pain in my achilles came back and I couldn't do it. So it was back to the gym and the exercise bike. I was destroyed again. I was so close, but I knew if I wasn't running now, two weeks before the race, I was in serious trouble.

I couldn't face the gym, so I went to the track to do my rehab exercises. I wanted to be with everyone else, to feel part of the team and get used to the humidity, but seeing my team-mates and the great shape they were in only frustrated me more.

I just had to plough on and keep believing that I could come good, and that I would come good.

I had to believe that a miracle could happen that would allow me to race and that I would then find something from somewhere that would enable me to win.

Chapter 13
Beijing 2008

**Two days before departing for Beijing I got another whisper
in my ear from a member of the management team, although
this was much more welcome than the one in Birmingham. Phil
Lane, the chef de mission, asked if I would carry the flag in the
opening ceremony.**

I was absolutely blown away. It is the greatest honour and all the
more special because your peers have chosen you to represent them.
That one conversation made every bit of heartache I had endured
over the previous five months seem worthwhile.

Phil said the plan was to fly to Beijing, have some photos taken in
front of the Bird's Nest Stadium, and then announce it to the press,
so could I keep it to myself and not tell anyone? Of course I was on
the phone home straight away telling Mum, Dad and a few friends,
and swearing them all to secrecy too.

The next day we flew to Beijing and went straight to the stadium to
have the official photos taken and to be interviewed by the BBC. It
was really blustery, but we found the perfect spot for the picture, just
outside the stadium.

Some security staff were putting barriers out and we were in their way. Security at the Beijing Games was incredibly strict, but we persuaded them to give us a few minutes to get the shot we needed. I was struggling to hold the flag in the wind so it was taking a while. Eventually one of the cameramen took his microphone off the boom pole and we attached the Union Jack to that as an impromptu flagpole.

We had the shot, the announcement was made and the picture went out across the internet, in newspapers and all over the world.

Soon the emails started coming in and we realised we had made a mistake. In our haste we had attached the Union Jack to the boom upside-down. People were writing to UK Athletics, the Paralympic Association and to me personally, accusing us of being disrespectful to the Royal family and to Great Britain. Apparently in naval terms, flying the flag the wrong way up would be seen as a sign of distress.

I guess the irony is that I was in distress, but I would never have been deliberately disrespectful. In 12 years of international athletics I was never prouder than when I wore the Union Jack.

To be honest, it was a small, cheap flag that we only had because I couldn't hold the big one. I'm sure most flags that size don't even have a right and wrong way up. Nevertheless I felt terrible about causing offence and the whole situation became yet another distraction.

The day of the opening ceremony arrived. Being me, I hadn't really planned too much. I was every bit as excited as I had been for the opening ceremonies in Sydney and Athens, but I was feeling apprehensive.

As the day went on, the excitement in the athletes' village built. The buses started arriving to take us to the stadium. We were told what time our bus would leave and I went off with a few mates to have something to eat before showering and getting ready.

I went back to the apartment and got my team uniform out. We were all wearing these blue trousers with deck shoes and white jackets. But when I went to put the trousers on, I realised they were flying quite high and stopped a few inches above my ankles. My team-mates found this hilarious. I was about to walk out for what was going to be the proudest moment of my life in front of a worldwide television audience of millions, but I was going to do it looking ridiculous.

At this point I was hoping someone else who would be less prominent during the ceremony might have helped. A good mate might have said, "Dan, you're front and centre, have my trousers." Not one offered.

We went to the kit room but there were no other trousers available, so I had to go as I was.

On the bus my mates were taking pictures of my ankles and they became the main talking point as we headed to the stadium. It was kind of funny, but I was starting to get wound up that I was going out onto this huge stage showing two inches of sock.

As at the two previous Games, there was about two hours of queuing before we even got to the stadium. I was messing about with my mates as we stood outside the stadium, watching the fireworks and the jets overhead.

I was having a laugh with John McFall, a leg-amputee sprinter, and Steffan Hughes, who was still Tracey Hinton's guide runner, when an official came over and led me away so I could be given the flag.

They took me to a room where all the flags were. I was fitted with a special harness and given a massive Union Jack. It was awesome.

I was also assigned an attractive Chinese lady to keep me company. I laid on some of my best Essex charm for her but that didn't work, so I just stood with her and waited while my mates were larking about and having a laugh.

My emotions were all over the place. I wanted to be with my mates but was overwhelmed by the honour of carrying the flag. Above all I was still really worried about my injury. We were still struggling to find a solution, but with just a week until my race, it was feeling like a losing battle.

I was also distracted by the fact Mum and Dad were not there. They had been to every international race I had ever competed in throughout my career. In Athens and Sydney they came to the opening and closing ceremonies too. But in Beijing they didn't manage to get opening ceremony tickets. When they booked I had been injured and we didn't know if I would be at the Games myself. Once we were certain I would be there it was too late and there were no tickets left.

I had a huge career highlight with this massive honour of carrying the flag, but was always conscious that this was the first thing I had ever done in my career that my parents wouldn't be there to share.

Victoria wasn't there either. Henry was only 10 months old at the time and we thought bringing him halfway round the world would involve too much upheaval. So she stayed at home to look after him and we decided Henry could come to London in 2012 and watch his dad race there instead.

As at previous Games, the build-up to the opening ceremony mostly involved standing around and joking, but when we got to the entrance to the track and heard, "Great Britain and Northern Ireland" over the public address, it really got me.

I walked out on the track, my heart pounding. Despite the uncertainty and setbacks, it was a huge high for me. I can't describe what it feels like to step out and have your team behind you. In all the photos I look really nervous. I probably was nervous – there were 80,000 watching me in the stadium and millions more on TV around the world – but, after making sure the flag was definitely the right way up, I enjoyed every minute of it.

My Essex boy reputation must have preceded me as well. I guess they had heard about my attempt to steal that duvet in Sydney because they made sure they took the flag straight off me the second I stepped off the track.

I sat down to enjoy the rest of the ceremony and, again, the lighting of the flame made me realise what was coming and what I was a part of. I had loved carrying the flag, but I needed to make sure that would not be my only contribution to the Beijing Paralympics.

The next day I went to see Neil Pollock, one of the team doctors. He'd looked after me all the way through and now he was doing whatever he could just to get me to the start line.

I told him I understood he was protecting me, but that I wouldn't be happy going into the heats without having run. I'd rather take the risk of pushing it in training if it meant I would be in a better condition when I got to the race.

They agreed to anaesthetise my achilles and soleus so I could try to run and we would see what happened. The belief was that my injuries were more neurological than physical. That meant, while pushing through the pain was not ideal, it was less likely to cause long-term damage than it would have done with a physical injury.

The medical team found the most remote possible part of the athletes' village so we could get away from everybody and train somewhere private. The last thing we wanted was for any of my opponents to see me trying to run with physios and doctors around me.

I started running slowly, steadily lengthening my strides. I felt fine and started to run, but as I eased off after just 30 or 40 metres I felt an almighty stabbing pain in my lower calf again. We all knew instantly that something had gone. I couldn't even walk, we had to get someone to come and pick me up in a buggy.

I was taken back to UK Athletics' medical room in the village where I stayed overnight, mainly so they could continue to treat me, but also so the rest of the team would not see my injury. We didn't want any rumours to start before there had been time for a proper diagnosis.

To give me the best chance of recovering in time to compete I was not allowed to move and had to have ice applied to my calf every four hours. Even during the night the physio set an alarm to wake herself up every four hours to keep icing my calf while I slept.

The next day there was no hiding as I went for yet another scan in the village's central medical facility, a temporary state-of-the-art hospital with two MRI scanners. As I made my way there, I was visibly limping with my lower leg heavily strapped. By now, word was getting round the village that I was in trouble.

The scan revealed a decent sized tear in my soleus, just six days before the race. There was no way I would be able to recover in time. The decision was made, it was over. I was out of the Paralympics.

We decided to keep it quiet for that day. We told the team officials and the relevant people from the Games organisers and I was officially withdrawn.

It was quite strange and I wasn't sure what to do with myself. I'd always been conscious that this could be my last Paralympics. At 35 years old I was the second oldest track and field athlete out there. The average age of the team was probably about 24 and I suddenly felt I didn't have much in common with the other athletes anymore.

Once we had made the decision it felt like a weight had been lifted. I wasn't relieved not to be running, but at least we had a result. Although it wasn't the result I wanted there was no more uncertainty and, for the first time that year, I knew what was going to happen.

I called Ayo to tell him and he was gutted. Then I had to call Mum and Dad, who were due to fly out a couple of days later. I'd decided I needed to go home. The team had said I could stay but I couldn't face being so near to the Games without really being a part of it. As a senior athlete, one of my roles was to mentor the younger athletes but I worried that all I would do was bring them down.

So I didn't just have to tell Mum and Dad I wouldn't be competing, I also had to tell them I would be gone by the time they got here. They decided that they would still fly out. Mum really wanted to see the Bird's Nest and it was just unfortunate that I wouldn't be competing in it when they got there.

I then had to make my last visit to the stadium, to announce my retirement during the BBC coverage of the Games. They had been fantastic to me throughout my career, we had done a lot of work together, which had given me the platform to build my profile. Speaking to them then was the last thing I wanted to do, but I felt I had to repay that.

While I was in the studio waiting to be interviewed, a 1500-metre race for my class – the T46 – was going on behind me. A lot of the athletes who would also run the 800 metres were out on the track and I could see they all looked fast. Not only was I going home, I now realised my world record was in trouble too. It was another gut blow.

If 2008 had gone well, I had considered running the 1500 metres as well, but instead I spent the heats for that event in a TV studio having to tell everyone that I wouldn't even be running the 800 metres.

The news had spread round the team and the camp and quite a few athletes came to find me to sympathise, but I just didn't want to be there. The next day I flew home. When I left the accommodation I brought the clothes from the opening ceremony (badly fitting trousers and all) but I left my athletics kit there. I hadn't earned it after all. I told the rest of the athletes, "if you want it, you can have it." And headed off to the village's transport terminal.

I could not have felt more lonely as I got on the next bus to the airport. The Games were only two days old at this point so nobody else was leaving. Apart from a young Chinese chaperone sent to look after me, I was the only person on the bus.

When I got to the airport I was pretty much alone in departures too. I was in the biggest airport in the world but my injury meant I couldn't even get up to take a walk and have a look around. I just sat there, not knowing what to do with myself.

Suddenly I heard someone shout, "Oi, Danny!"

Of all people, it was Richard Wilson, the actor who played Victor Meldrew in *One Foot in the Grave*. He is a keen supporter of the Paralympics and I had met him once before. He had gone out to China to watch some of the Games.

He asked what I was doing there, so I stood in the middle of Beijing Airport explaining to Victor Meldrew why I was going home early. It was all a bit odd.

As we said our goodbyes I said that I probably wouldn't see him again. I thought when we got on the plane he would turn left while I went to the right to sit in the cheap seats.

I boarded the plane and went to the back to sit down. There I bumped into some other members of our management team who I didn't know were going to be on the flight.

While we were chatting a stewardess came over and told me someone at the front of the plane had said I might be more comfortable up there, so I was led up to first class after all. I didn't see Richard Wilson when I got there – I can only assume he was even further forward – but I was hugely grateful for his gesture.

The journey was at least more comfortable, although I was aware that my flight would have passed Mum and Dad coming the other way, flying out to watch a race that I wouldn't be in.

I was picked up at the airport by Victoria's dad, Peter. Coming home was tough. At least I had Henry, who wasn't yet a year old, to keep me busy.

I wanted to stay as far away from the Paralympics as possible so Victoria and I booked a cottage in Somerset for a week and went down there with Henry to get away from it all.

We were there by the time of the Men's T46 800 metres final, but I didn't watch it. I couldn't bring myself to, although I couldn't help checking the result on the internet that night. Of course my world record had gone, and it had gone to Marcin Awiżeń, an athlete who had never beaten me on the track. He shaved 0.07 seconds off my best time.

The most frustrating thing was that we never got to the bottom of what had gone wrong that year. There were all sorts of ifs and buts. What if I had changed our approach sooner? Or could I have done anything else differently?

I don't think I'll ever know the answer, or even if there is an answer.

It should have been my year but, for whatever reason, it wasn't.

My outlook on life has always been to look to the future. I have never spent too long worrying about what has already happened and am always quick to look for the next thing. In the past this had sometimes been detrimental. After winning in Athens, Ayo had to tell me to just enjoy what I had done for once.

I had come out of the Athens Games thinking I had two choices: I could either rest, satisfied with my victory, and spend the next 20 or so years just telling people about my achievement; or I could move on to the next thing and try to achieve some more.

Now, four years later, the result was different but the choices were the same: I could either dwell on what had happened and spend years moaning about my bad luck; or I could move on to the next challenge and try to make the most of that.

What happened in Beijing was a huge dent to my confidence, but I didn't ever think my career was over. Instead I was already thinking about what I needed to do to get back.

There would be more hurdles to get past though. First I had my funding review. I had built up a few sponsorship deals in the build-up to Beijing and they all featured win bonuses that I obviously never received.

Also, all the sponsors tended to work on a four-year cycle so they were starting to look to the next Paralympics, London 2012. Luckily I had a couple of local sponsors who did stay with me, but I lost the majority of my deals.

As a result I needed to hang on to whatever I could of my lottery funding, but when that was reviewed I was struck off completely. I was in London, about to attend an event for the British Paralympic Association, when I got the phone call from UK Athletics. I stood on the Embankment and stared at the Thames, not knowing what to do.

I rang Phil Lane and told him I couldn't come to the event after all, caught the train home and tried to think about what to do next.

For the first time in my career I had no lottery funding at all. At a time when I needed the help and support more than ever, just about all my financial backing dried up.

I was still injured and needing rehab. The season was over but at a time when my colleagues would be enjoying a break, I was having to do the rehab I most hated.

The decision to pull my funding had been taken by someone calculating an arbitrary time that they thought would win gold in London. The same person then decided that, as I would be 39 years old by then, I would not be able to achieve that time. That one person subsequently left UK Athletics as a new performance manager came in and got rid of a lot of people, but the damage had already been done.

At least there was now an appeals process in place, so I gathered a lot of data together to show that the London final might not be as quick as they had anticipated and that 39-year-olds can still win major medals.

It was finally agreed I had been in such good shape earlier that year – before picking up the injury – that I deserved to maintain some funding.

My lottery cash was restored but at a lower level and only for an initial six months. That would at least get me through the winter and ensure I had access to whatever treatment I needed. But if my funding was going to continue beyond then, I had to prove by summer 2009 that I was back in world class shape.

I once again had something to aim for: to show that I wasn't finished at 35 and could still compete.

2008 had been a disaster, but it was in the past and I was looking forward again.

1) *Pre-Athens training camp, Cyprus (the endurance squad).*

2) *Dressed to impress (ready for the opening ceremony, Athens 2004).*

3) *Grabbing lunch (athletes' village).*

1) *The nervous wait.*

2) *Feeling comfortable at 300m.*

3) *Crossing the finish line.*

4) *Magic moments.*

5) *Can't believe I finally did it!*

6) *Lap of honour.*

1) *Post-race with Victoria.*

2) *Standing on the podium.*

3) *A proud mum.*

4) *Now let the party begin.*

5) *Olympic announcement, Trafalgar Square 2005.*

1+2) *Finally hitched*
(our wedding day, December 2006).

3+4) *Warm weather training in*
South Africa.

5) *Olympic Torch Relay 2008.*

6) *A proud moment (carrying the flag*
at the opening ceremony, Beijing 2008).

1) *I can't pedal any further (Chris Moore, 900 miles into the Deloitte Ride Across Britain).*

2) *Open road (with Steve and Chris).*

3) *Another finish line crossed (with Red Ted, Henry's class mascot).*

Chapter 14
The home straight

I knew I would find it tough to win medals in London, but I definitely hadn't made the decision to retire. After the frustration of having to work through the winter while all the other athletes were enjoying a break, I came back feeling great.

In January the times I was running in training maintained my low-level funding until the summer. I could now focus all my energy into the Paralympic World Cup, which would take place in Manchester in May. It was the first big international meeting of the season and would be my only chance to post a decent time before my six months' temporary support came to an end.

I knew my funding would disappear to nothing if I was not quick enough in Manchester. It probably should have felt like a last chance, but I was feeling mentally and physically strong and was confident I had nothing to worry about.

Four weeks before the Paralympic World Cup was due to start, I was doing a standard training session. I had been set 20 repetitions of 200 metres with 30 seconds recovery time between each one. It was an innocuous routine that I had done hundreds of times before. I was running slowly and not overstretching, but on the third repetition, halfway round the bend, I felt a sharp stabbing pain in the back of my left leg.

I went in to the physio knowing I had damaged my hamstring, but hoping it was not too bad.

A couple of days later a scan revealed a grade-two minor tear. The average repair team for that injury was several weeks but I only had one month until my race. The race that was going to prove I wasn't just an old, has-been who was going to get injured all the time.

I managed to get back running and made it to the start line, desperate to prove that I was still a world-class athlete. Getting that far was a feat in itself, but I knew I hadn't had time to go through the proper race preparation. I had rarely felt so much pressure.

Some of the best athletes in the world were there and it felt good to line up alongside the elite again. The gun went off and I was quickly into my stride, moving easily with no trouble. I went through the bell comfortably in third place, well in touch with the leaders. Approaching the 600-metre mark I went to attack. I kicked on, moving up to second as we took the final bend.

From nowhere I felt that pain in my hamstring again. For the first time in my career I tumbled to the track. I just sat there, wide-eyed, watching the race's climax unfold in front of me. I realised there and then that my career was over.

I knew I had come back too hard and fast, but had taken the risk of racing too early in a desperate bid to prove that I could still compete at that level. It had backfired. What was frustrating was that this was a completely new injury and had nothing to do with the problems I had come through in the build-up to Beijing the previous year.

I stayed in Manchester that night. The rest of the team had left, but I was told not to drive with a torn hamstring. There was only me and the team's performance coach, Peter Eriksson, left in the hotel. As we sat and chatted, our conversation turned to what I could do for my post-racing career. Peter suggested some mentoring work, telling me there would always be a position for me at UK Athletics.

When I got home I did some serious soul searching. I still loved running, but I didn't seem to be spending much time on the track these days.

The lure of London 2012 was huge, a once-in-a-lifetime chance to compete in a Paralympic Games in my home city, but I knew that to get there I might have to take another three years of the mental torment that athletics had put me through over the previous 12 months.

I also wondered if just getting to London would be enough. Would I be happy standing on that start line, knowing in the back of my mind that I almost certainly wouldn't win and possibly wouldn't even get a medal? I might have been fighting just to make the final. Having been the world number one, I wasn't sure if I could settle for that.

At the age of 36, after 11 years of international athletics, I decided I was prepared to call it a day.

But I wasn't yet ready to give up my final dream of retiring in front of a home crowd, so I found myself back in rehab.

There was a Grand Prix event scheduled at Crystal Palace Stadium on 25 July 2009 which I earmarked for my farewell appearance. Knowing it would be my last race, the organisers invited my main competitors from around the world to ensure I got a fitting send off.

The date was set and all I had to do was make sure I was fit enough to run.

Ayo really held me back and restricted me to light training. If I did anything too strenuous the risk of reinjury would be too high. I just had to make the start line and then run 800 metres without getting injured.

I topped up my training with a few more sessions on the bike. I would still go out regularly with my neighbour, Chris Spooner, and the route we usually took went over a ford. I always used to get off and push my bike around the ford – over a footbridge – while Chris would just ride through it. I don't know why, but in the build-up to my retirement race I decided I was going to have a go at the ford myself, so I went for it.

As Chris hit the water the spray came up and hit my face. I turned to dodge it, my slick tyres hit the sludge at the bottom of the ford and I came off, skidding through the water on my back until I found myself laying in the road as Chris rolled up with laughter.

I had a nasty gash down from my knee and a broken bone in my hand. Luckily the leg injury was not serious – although I still have the scar – and a broken hand wasn't going to stop me running, however painful it was.

When the day of the race arrived I was fit enough to run, but was not prepared at all. It was quite a strange feeling. I wasn't as nervous as I used to get because I wasn't going out to win the race, just to say goodbye, but I was feeling emotional.

I knew my family were all on their way to watch me. Victoria was bringing Henry along, which was a really big thing for me. He wasn't even two yet but, even if he didn't remember it, I wanted him to have seen his dad running in a Great Britain kit.

Ever since he had been alive I hadn't really done myself justice. The only time he'd watched me compete was in Manchester, where all he had seen was me sitting on the track while everyone else ran.

As I was trying to go through my final preparation in Crystal Palace, I seemed to be constantly on the phone to Victoria. She was lost somewhere with her mum and Henry in the car. There were huge traffic problems across London that day and, as the race approached, Mum and Dad and Paul and several others all got stuck and were nowhere near the stadium.

It felt like nobody was going to get there to see my final race. At the very last moment, just as I was going into the pre-race, call room procedure, Victoria called to say she had arrived and that my mum, dad and brother were there already.

Just standing on the start line I had this warm feeling. It was a big crowd and I'd always had this dream that when I retired, it would be on a home track. This was the second best thing to bowing out at London 2012.

The gun went off and the race went smoothly. I was moving freely in a good position. I was in second place behind the Kenyan Abraham Tarbei with about 200 metres to go, but as I came round onto the home straight, with 120 metres or so to run, the lack of training and preparation hit me like a brick wall. Tarbei just strode ahead and pulled away as my legs got heavier.

Then what might have been the most amazing event of my entire career happened. Marcin Awiżeń, the Polish athlete who had taken my world record in Beijing, came up beside me on the home straight. He must have sensed I was struggling and lacking fitness.

As a professional athlete his instinct would undoubtedly have been to run off and destroy me, trying to win the race. Instead he ran alongside me all the way down the home straight, shouting at me all the time as he ran, "Come on, Dan, you can do this," and, "Faster, faster, come on."

He called me all the way to the finish line. Although he dipped me when we got there to ensure he beat me to second.

That was quite telling about him as a person. To do that, especially when there was prize money available, was quite special.

I was really pleased for myself too. I had stepped onto a track in a Great Britain vest for the very last time, competed against the best athletes in the world, and finished third.

After the race I went on a lap of honour and had an interview over the stadium public address. I had thought so often about what that moment would feel like, but you can't plan for it at all – it just felt surreal.

I came home and spent a bit of time with my family, but I still had one little dream to fulfil. I had started running for Thurrock Harriers when I was nine years old. I was now retired from international athletics but I thought one last race in a Thurrock vest would be the perfect way to finish my career.

I spoke to the club and ended up going to a wet and windy league match in Basingstoke, where I ran the 800 metres and won the race.

Dave Staines, the team manager, had been trying to get me to run a 1500 metres for years. I had run the distance as a child, but as an international athlete I had always concentrated on my own event – either the 400 or the 800 metres.

As I wasn't an international athlete any more I thought, "why not?"

I asked Dave if he had anyone lined up to run the 1500 metres.

"Well, I have," he said, "but you're quicker."

I asked him, "Do you want me to do the 15?"

"That would be very kind. I've already put your name down."

That day I ran a personal best time over the distance, finishing second in 4 minutes, 12 seconds.

But I wasn't finished there. I went on to run the 4 x 400 metre relay, which we won as a team. As they had been so many times before, Mum and Dad were there in the driving rain to watch me go out as a winner.

Thurrock wanted me to race for them regularly, but I stuck to my guns and retired. I had really enjoyed running that day, but I knew the only way I was going to go was slower.

Chapter 15
Life after running

My next big challenge was adjusting to being a retired athlete and just getting used to not running.

Victoria and my family had been warned that I would be susceptible to depression. My life had been so structured for the previous 11 years, I had goals and every day I was trying to do something better. All of a sudden I had nothing any more.

For the first few weeks it was great. I drank as much alcohol and ate as much unhealthy food as I could, but it quickly became apparent that was never going to be enough and I needed something back in my life.

I struggled for a while after retiring. It took some time for the depression to hit but when it did I was really low. I just didn't know what to do with myself. Having been so focused for over a decade, I couldn't just switch that off.

I still had my motivational speaking career of course. I had been steadily getting busier since starting that just after Sydney. In the latter part of my athletics career I had travelled further afield and had even had bookings to speak across Europe and in Dubai and Malaysia.

While I was running, all speaking engagements had to be fitted in around my athletics. This was even more of a challenge as I started to get international bookings and I had to turn some of them down as training or events got in the way. I told myself that when I stopped running, I would take all the bookings available and announce myself as an international speaker.

When I retired I put everything into the speaking to try to make that happen. Of course, that was exactly the time the global recession hit. As companies made cutbacks, paying for motivational speakers became less of a priority for them and there wasn't much work here or abroad.

For a while the transition into full time speaking was not as smooth as I had hoped. I managed to tick along though and now, as London 2012 approaches, I am getting busier than ever.

It's strange, but speaking is something I am really passionate about. I get the same buzz from delivering my speeches that I used to get from competing. I get the same nervousness before I go on stage, and the same exhilaration when I know I have delivered a good speech.

Whether I'm talking to a massive, blue-chip company or a school awards ceremony, I want to be better than every other speaker they have ever had.

The other dream I had was that I would get back onto the rugby pitch. I wanted to retire from athletics young enough that I could go back to the game.

I had played for Thurrock all my life, but I had moved from Corringham to the other end of Essex since my last game and Thurrock was hardly my local team anymore, so I joined Maldon Rugby Club just before Christmas 2009.

When I had quit playing 12 years before, I had put all my kit in a bag in my parents' loft. The bag stayed there until I joined Maldon, so I walked into the club without knowing anyone and wearing kit that was over a decade out of date. The reaction of my team-mates when I turned up for my first training session let me know that the game had changed quite a bit since I last played.

When I had come back to play for Thurrock for the first time after the crash, I had gone through six months of training before I even considered stepping onto the pitch. This time I did one session before deciding I was ready.

I walked out to represent Maldon's third team on a cold Saturday, threw myself into a tackle early on, injured my shoulder and was ruled out of playing for the next four weeks.

I have stayed fairly injury-free since then and still love the game, although I have had to adjust my expectations since retiring as a professional sportsman. I'd only been at Maldon a few weeks when the captain was going round the changing room, asking all the players if they would be available for the game next week.

Player after player replied, "I can't, the missus says I've got to go Christmas shopping."

At first I couldn't believe they were missing rugby to go shopping, but I suddenly thought, "This is what's in store for me now."

All the times Victoria had tried to drag me out shopping, or to her best friend's cousin's wedding, only to be told that there was a big event coming up and my training had to come first. It suddenly dawned on me that, from now on, she might get her own way. I might end up being dragged round the shops myself or having to go to some of these weddings of people I'd never met.

It also took me a while to get back into the team mentality. When I first took up athletics I had struggled because I was so used to being part of a team. Over my career I developed the individual mentality that was needed in athletics. But I brought that with me to my early Maldon rugby career. It felt wrong joining in any victory celebrations if I personally hadn't played well. I was coming off the pitch frustrated even if we'd won.

I've now got used to playing as a team – and winning and losing as a team – but I am still getting used to the fact that I am simply not as good as I used to be.

When I was 21 I had more of the aggression that you need to play rugby. By the time I was 36 I was also three stone lighter and tended to bounce off the players I was trying to tackle. I learned slowly that rugby would now have to be more about fun than winning.

I have also filled my days picking up bits of work on local TV and radio. I was covering Olympics stories for *BBC Look East* for a while. My TV work has slowly built up and I worked as a pundit for Channel 4, covering the World Athletics championships in New Zealand and the Paralympic World Cup.

I hope to be involved in the coverage of the London Paralympics too, although I would still rather be on the track. It's far more nerve-racking going in front of a live camera than it is standing on the start line of a major championships final.

It didn't happen often, but when I was running, there was nothing more infuriating than one of the commentators or presenters getting even a tiny detail wrong and broadcasting it to the nation. Now I work really hard to make sure I know every last bit of information about all the competitors so I don't make any mistakes. They are international athletes and deserve that respect.

Plus, I guess my approach to talking about running is the same as my approach to running itself, the same as my approach to public speaking and the same as my approach to everything in life: whatever I am doing, I want to be the best at it.

I was once doing a conference with lots of Olympians, including Sir Steve Redgrave, Steve Backley and Steve Cram. Someone asked us who our inspirations were?

Steve Cram just said, "I never wanted to be like anybody else. I just wanted to win."

I got that instantly. I thought, "That is me."

That attitude served me well in my running career but in everyday life it can drive those around me mad. On honeymoon with Victoria, we were floating around in a little sailing dinghy just off Zanzibar under a clear, blue sky. It was idyllic, but I started to get agitated that our sail was flapping a bit and we weren't going as fast as another honeymooning couple in a different boat.

It was that need to win that kept me driving and pushing myself to the top throughout my career. Even after I had won gold in Athens, the first thing I said to Ayo was that I thought I could have gone quicker.

I am often asked if I am satisfied with my athletics career. Of course I am pleased with what I achieved, but I cannot honestly say I am satisfied. I would have liked more titles, to take my world record a bit lower, and especially to have been able to compete at London 2012. I always want more, but I think that is a characteristic of all top athletes.

Retirement for me has been largely about finding new outlets for that drive. Obviously TV, rugby and my speaking have given me that, and I soon had another distraction to keep me busy as my second son, Albert, was born on 16 April 2010.

Unlike Henry, Albert managed to arrive on time and Victoria and I were much better prepared. This time his bedroom was ready, the car seat was fitted and everything went smoothly.

I could never have imagined how fulfilled having two boys would make me feel. After everything I have been through and everything I have achieved it really is the icing on the cake.

Having two healthy sons just blows me away. I only hope they get as much enjoyment from sport as I have in my life. If they go on to achieve anything in sport, that's great – of course I would love that – but really I just want them to enjoy playing. I can't wait to be standing on a touchline in the pouring rain on a January afternoon, watching them play rugby. If nothing else, I'll have someone else to go training with, although I may have to wait a few years for that.

Despite having my hands full at home, and channelling what energy I had left into speaking, TV work and rugby, I still found I was missing training. I am actually quite lazy and I couldn't find a reason to run. I would go for the occasional jog, but I needed something to focus on to make me get out there and train properly.

In summer 2010 I heard about the Deloitte Ride Across Britain, a nine-day cycle ride from John O'Groats to Land's End scheduled to take place the next year, which was organised to raise money for Paralympics GB.

I knew a few people at Paralympics GB so I told them if they wanted me, I would be available.

I hadn't heard anything by autumn, so I started training for the following year's London Marathon, a box I have always wanted to tick. I hadn't been able to run the event while I was a professional athlete and I thought it would be best to do it soon after retiring, while I was still reasonably fit. SportsAid asked me to take part as one of their team captains. That was all the incentive I needed.

Three weeks later, in November 2010, I got the phone call from Paralympics GB, asking me to be their ambassador for the Ride Across Britain. It felt like too good an opportunity to miss.

But I wasn't going to do it alone and there was only one person I wanted to invite along with me. I went straight next door to my old training partner, Chris, and asked how he fancied riding from John O'Groats to Land's End?

At this stage I hadn't officially signed up myself, but Chris went straight online, registered himself and paid his deposit.

"You'd better bloody come with me," he said.

Once again, Chris was streets ahead of me in training, helped by him buying a shiny new road bike while I struggled along on my old mountain bike. But in January 2011 I was supplied with my own shiny new Boardman bike, which I had modified by the Paralympic cycling team. Chris and I couldn't resist having a tinker too and modified it a bit further. Soon I was pushing him all the way again.

I was finding it very difficult to train though. Chris was still cycling into work and back every day so he was in pretty good shape and he just went on a few longer rides to make sure he was ready.

But I was still training for the Marathon and was out running most nights. It got to March, one month before the Marathon, and I started to get a bit of trouble with my knees. Trying to get my body into a condition where it would be capable of running 26 miles and cycling 100 miles a day for nine days was proving too much. I made the decision to put all my energy into getting ready for the ride. SportsAid generously let me delay running the Marathon by a year.

On 10 June, we flew up to Wick and got a taxi to John O'Groats where we would meet our bikes.

It was an absolutely beautiful day as everybody lined up at the start. As an ambassador I needed to be at the front to have my photo taken at the start line but, as usual, I was running late. Everybody was waiting to go as I came charging up from the back yelling, "wait for me."

I got to the front and the starter asked if I was ready. I said, "No, I just need to put my glove on."

But she ignored me and shouted, "Go!"

I quickly jumped on my bike, pulling my glove on with my teeth. Sarah Storey, one of the Paralympic cyclists, was also there as an ambassador and was alongside me for the photos. In my hurry to get going I nearly clipped her wheel. I swerved to avoid her and ended up crashing the bike. Three metres into a 950-mile bike ride and I had already fallen off. In front of everybody. Luckily I managed to stay in the saddle for the rest of the 949 and a bit miles.

The first day was amazing although, like everyone else, we went off too fast. By day three, Chris and I had hooked up with a couple of other riders, Steve Girdler and Chris Moore from Adecco. We stayed with them for the whole of the rest of the trip and had a great time.

After the beautiful weather at the start, it rained from midway through day two until we got to Land's End, but we loved every minute of it. We cycled between 90 and 120 miles every day and then camped out in the evening. Chris and I had set out with the sole aim of enjoying ourselves so we never rushed, we just pootled along and had a laugh. Not once did I even think, "I wish I wasn't doing this."

There were two scheduled pit stops on each leg where we could pick up food and drink, but we added a few stops of our own, filling up with pork pies to keep us going. We actually gained weight during the trip.

The four of us had a blast. Everyone else on the trip would say they knew when we were coming because they'd hear us laughing before they could see us.

The sheer effort of trying to steer a bike and stay upright, putting all that pressure through one arm, was exhausting. I couldn't feel my fingers by day three and was struggling to do my zips up. By day six I was really starting to suffer. I couldn't carry my bags or do anything with my hand beyond holding the handlebar and changing gear. Towards the end of the day even that would be difficult.

Everyone was struggling. You can't undertake a bike ride from John O'Groats to Land's End without expecting a challenge. By day eight, Chris Moore's knees were playing up so we had to ease off the pace, but we stayed together as a group and had developed a camaraderie that helped us all through.

The last three days – through the hills of Dorset, Devon and Cornwall – were the toughest. But we made it to the last day and a final 90-mile blast into Land's End. I remember the four of us standing on the start line preparing for a momentous last day, knowing that it was only those 90 miles between us and the end of our ride.

On the final day I even attacked a cattle grid for the first time. I remembered breaking my hand crossing a ford while training for my farewell race, and had convinced myself the same would happen again if I tried to cycle over a cattle grid.

There had been a lot of grids in Scotland and, for each one, I got off and pushed my bike around it while all the other cyclists shot past. I lost about 400 metres at every grid and would have to make it up each time, but I couldn't bring myself to cycle over them.

As we crossed Bodmin Moor on that last leg, I saw the first cattle grid for six days. I was so tired I decided I couldn't be bothered going around them any more so I just went for it. Straight away I wished I had done that from the start.

Chris Spooner, Chris Moore and I then stopped seven miles from the finish so I could put my t-shirt on ready for the photos as I crossed the line. Steve had gone ahead by this stage and had already finished.

There was a young lad riding this elliptical bike on the ride. It was a strange device that looked like a cross trainer on wheels. He had ridden it the whole way to set a record for the furthest distance anyone had been on one of these bikes. He whizzed past as I was putting my t-shirt on.

I knew that he would have photos taken as he crossed the line but, as an ambassador, I was having photos taken too. I didn't want to take anything away from him – he was a young lad and was about to set a world record – so I thought I should make sure we didn't cross the line too close together.

Common sense would have told me to just hang back and let him have his moment. Unfortunately idiot sense took over, so I got the two Chrisses back on their bikes and we were off in pursuit of this lad on his elliptical bike.

We blasted the last seven miles to try to beat him into Land's End. We passed him but, of course, when he saw us go past, he stepped it up too. He was on a high as he came to the end of a fantastic achievement and was happy to give us a race. Eventually we shook him off and managed to lose him.

As Chris Spooner and I came to the top of a hill very near the end we noticed Chris Moore was no longer with us. Chris Spooner looked behind us and swore loudly, "He's only overtaking a car!"

And there he was, knees shot to pieces, but giving it everything he had to get to the finish.

We came into Land's End so fast we only just managed to stop before we hit the water. It was an amazing feeling, thinking about what we had achieved. I will always remember the experience and would love to do something similar in the future.

I do have the London Marathon to come. I think the bike ride will be hard to top but then, who knows what else life still has in store for me?

I guess I have been through a lot, but I still believe everything happens for a reason and life hasn't yet given me a challenge that I couldn't overcome.

Many of the things life has thrown at me have taken me off my chosen path, but I have never been scared to change direction. Events in my life may have shut down one dream, but there has always been a new dream to pursue.

Often that new dream has turned out to be more fulfilling than whatever I was working towards before.

I believe all our lives are full of defining moments. Some are thrust upon us, but others are results of decisions we have made in our lives. Wherever you find yourself, you can't worry about how you got there, you just need to think about where you're going next.

I have won gold medals and travelled the world in a career that has surpassed all my expectations, but my defining moment was a car crash.

I didn't choose to lose my arm, but after it happened I chose not to let life drift along without me. I chose to play that first game of rugby, it was televised, someone realised I used to be an athlete, asked me to run for them and, with a lot of love and support from my friends and family, a whole new career opened up for me.

I don't know what's coming next. My life has taken many twists and turns and I'm sure it will take more. All I do know is that everything I have been through so far has ultimately worked out pretty well.